Block Panchayaths as Change Agents in India's Decentralisation

Block Panchayaths as Change Agents in India's Decentralisation:

The Kerala Experience

Manju S. Nair

Saisree K.G. & Vijayasree R.M.

KALPAZ

ISBN: 978-93-5324-301-2 (HB)

First Published, 2020

Published by

Kalpaz Publications
C-30, Satyawati Nagar,
Delhi – 110052
Ph.: 011-47034999, 9811692060
www.kalpazpublications.com
E-mail: kalpaz@hotmail.com

Printed at: G. Print Process, Delhi

Dedication

Dedicated to my father, Sri. M. Rajasekharan Nair who has been the source of incredible support, guidance and motivation for me and my students

— **Manju S. Nair**

Contents

Foreword

The success story of Nedumangad Block Panchayath, Kerala is highly inspiring for all those who look forward to the prospects of democratic decentralisation in the state. The primary proof of the success of the Panchayath is the overwhelming participation of the citizenry in development planning, right from the early stages of planning such as preparatory studies and project formulation to the final stages such as operationalization and social auditing. Participation has not been limited to people who directly or indirectly benefited from the projects implemented. On the contrary, people have come forward and participated in large numbers for the common good. Further, the initiatives of the Panchayath are proving to be sustainable too. It is not surprising, therefore, that the Block Panchayath has won acclaims and state and national awards in consecutive years for its achievements. As can be expected it is now attracting development scholars as well who undertake in-depth studies on various aspects of participatory planning and governance at the local level. Importance of research on such development experiments can hardly be exaggerated. The study by Manju S. Nair, Saisree K.G. and Vijayasree R.M. is an important contribution to the relevant literature.

First of all, this study is a valuable documentation of the multifaceted development experiment undertaken by the Nedumangad Block Panchayath. Secondly, with the help of a thorough and critical analysis of the projects and their outcomes it attempts an objective evaluation of the Nedumangad experiment. Thirdly, the study delineates the factors that had contributed to the success of the projects implemented by the Panchayaths. In the process it also draws important lessons to be learnt and emulated. Another contribution of notable academic value is the attempt to revisit the redundancy hypothesis pertaining to the middle tier of the three tier architecture of rural local governments in Kerala.

As the authors argue there is persistent confusion regarding the role of Block Panchayaths in the multi-tier arrangement of governance in the state. It is true that the problem of lack of role-clarity is highest in the case of the Block Panchayaths. But, it is a subset of a larger problem of the distribution of powers and responsibilities across different agencies. The task of arriving at the right architecture of the distribution of powers, resources and responsibilities across different tiers of government so that the democratic state apparatus functions in the most effective manner is not yet fully done. In fact, the right combination can be arrived only through praxis. It is here the Nedumangad experiment and the present study assumes special value. As the authors argue Nedumangad Block Panchayath has successfully carved out a space for itself which is in harmony with other agencies and tiers of government. The lessons of this experiment therefore will be of immense use for other regions in the country. It should also inform future attempts to improve upon the relevant Acts in the state.

The effort to establish a distinct and relatively uncontested role for the Block Panchayath succeeded mainly because of the focus on hitherto neglected areas such as agriculture and allied activities and protection of environment. The decision of the Block Panchayath to abstain from individual beneficiary oriented projects would have also helped in ensuring complementarity vis-à-vis projects undertaken by the lower tier. In other words the focus on the larger picture helped in a big way.

The study brings out a picture of successful integration of varied agencies in the projects implemented in the Block. The process of integration is not confined to the three tiers of rural local governments. The line departments of the state government, agencies implementing centrally sponsored programmes, voluntary organisations, community associations, neighbourhood groups, cooperative institutions, etc., appear to have worked together in addressing local development problems. This certainly is a commendable achievement wherein the local government has acted as a fulcrum of integration. In hindsight this was one of the expected positive spill-over effects of democratic decentralisation.

As a review of studies on people's planning in the state would reveal a major limitation of the experiment has been the inability to improve and show tangible results in the productive sector. This failure was noted in the goods producing sectors in general, in industry as well as agriculture and allied sectors. The more recent period appears to have changed the pattern. There are some clear signs of change at least in the primary sector. As the study clearly brings out the experience of Nedumangad Block Panchayath shows how things can be improved in the productive sectors. In agriculture, fragmentation of holdings and atomisation of farming have been a major debilitating factor. It has drained the bargaining power of the peasants in various markets in a big way besides imposing scale disadvantages. The Block Panchayath appears to have addressed this problem by bringing together the farms as well as the farmers. It has successfully aggregated the power of the atomised farmers to their advantage. After all this is what the people expects from their governments. The governments at all levels should be able to empower the people by bringing them together.

Finally, in my opinion the study underlines the need to undertake serious research on the excellent work done by the local governments in the state. Undoubtedly the people and the local governments have evolved many successful development models. It is important to follow up such good work by undertaking research so that the lessons to be learnt are picked up and added to the body of existing knowledge in the relevant discipline. The continuity of 'doing and learning and doing' should be sustained unfettered.

Dr. K.N. Harilal

Member

Kerala State Planning Board

Preface

Decentralised administrative structure in India generally has a three-tier classification, with Gram Panchayaths at the grassroot level, Block Panchayaths at the intermediate level and District Panchayaths at the top level, with Kerala following the same pattern. However, considering the limited geographic terrain of the state and the kind of administrative needs of the society, several studies points out the intermediate tier to be redundant in functioning, owing to the fact that the functioning of Block Panchayaths in Kerala fail at a point where the statutory characteristics of the level are breached for convenience in execution and where the functional role is rarely distinguished from that of other tiers. In this context, Block Panchayaths should have a marked deviation from the current practice of replicating the activities of Gram Panchayaths,to becoming an innovator in productive and social front, so as to achieve inclusive, equitable and sustainable development and act as change agents.

However, against the background of instances of inadequacies in the functioning of Block Panchayaths as an intermediate tier; a generalised judgement cannot be formed on its redundancy. Nedumangad Block Panchayath, in Thiruvananthapuram district of Kerala, stands out as a case with replicable merits, by effectively performing the specified general and sectoral functions assigned to a Block Panchayath through an optimal mix of good governance, resource management and people's participation. The book 'Block Panchayaths as Change Agents in India's Decentralisation: The Kerala Experience' is an analytical exposition of the importance of decentralisation at block level, illustrated through the relevant case of Nedumangad Block Panchayath, wherein the multiple facets behind the successful functioning of the particular Block Panchayath is identified and analysed. A conceptual and practical framework integrating elements of good governance, Environmental Governance and sustainability is used in the study.

Nedumangad Block Panchayath initiated a spectrum of interventions under the umbrella scheme- "SAMRUDHI" (Sustainable Agricultural Management and Rural Development Initiative), which includes innovative schemes and projects in agriculture, health, education and rural infrastructure front. The philosophy of good environmental governance, whereby individual and collective actions are managed in pursuance of environmental goods and related societal outcomes, is embedded in the schemes designed and implemented by Nedumanagad Block Panchayath. The major schemes initiated are:-

- VallamNira, a project for nutritional self-sufficiency at household level
- Jaivagramam, a model Bio village reiterating organic practices
- Jyothirgamaya Balya, ensuring preventive and curative care for children
- Jyothirgamaya Kaumara, giving health education, social orientation and health care facilities for young adults and parents.
- Maramath, Strengthening infrastructural base through Public works
- Killiyar Protection, extending the activities of block to rejuvenation of Killi river through participatory approach
- Agri-Incubation Centre, providing training and support to women entrepreneurs in Agri-food processing sector
- Projects strengthening the socio-cultural fabrics of the locality and creating sustainable livelihoods

It is observed that the successful functioning of Nedumangad Block Panchayath traced during the four year period under consideration of the study is found to be rooted in the administration performing in alignment with the statutory provisions, enabling the

Block Panchayath to have convergence with various tiers and other departments at state level, facilitating appropriate channelizing of funds and utilisation of expertise by various agencies. Further, the long-term sustainability of any intervention would depend on its economic legitimacy in the sense of the ability to make a perceptible difference to the general standard of living of the population, of the deprived sections in particular. Considering the performance of Nedumangad Block Panchayath; most of the projects and schemes that the Block Panchayath has formulated and implemented have a direct or indirect bearing upon the productive sectors, with agriculture as the pivot. Also, interventions are found to be made in sequential order, whereby multifold opportunities are generated and popularised. All the interventions by the Nedumangad Block Panchayath were made with a big picture of sustainability, conceived at economic, social and environmental front. Finally, the success of Nedumangad Block Panchayath shall be attributed to the political will and ability of administrative construct in identifying agents of change in all development areas. It is understood that the activities and schemes of Nedumangad Block Panchayath are in tune with the need of the hour and with a long-term achievable target of strengthening resource base, management of natural resources and consequently creating sustainable livelihood. In recognition to the sustained effort, the Nedumangad Block Panchayath has consecutively received the award for best Block Panchayath, both at national and state level for 2017-18, 2018-19 and 2019-20.This book which is an analytical account of the identified challenges, needed interventions, actions and experiences of Nedumangad Block Panchayath will be mainly useful to researchers, academicians and practitioners to understand and appreciate the strength and potential of decentralisation particularly at intermediate level, in bringing out a progressive change to the society.

Manju S. Nair

Saisree K.G. and Vijayasree R.M

Acknowledgement

The initial idea regarding the book was conceived as a part of the visit that the authors had to Nedumangad Block Panchayath and the interview with the President Sri B. Biju. The visit was as a part of the course 'Agroecology: Action Learning and Research' organised in collaboration with Norwegian University of Life Sciences. We thank the whole Norwegian team, Prof. Geir Leiblein, Prof. Tor Arvid and Dr. Anna Marie Nicolayson for opening us the broad canvas of action research in Agroecology. Sri B. Biju - the dynamic president of the block is the person behind the successful functioning of the body, making it receive prestigious national and state awards. Watching his strenuous effort, we feel that it would be a serious default on academia, if we do not provide an analytical account in recognition of their activities, integrating it with the conceptual framework of sustainability and environmental governance. Placing on record, gratitude to the whole stakeholders of Decentralised governance in the State of Kerala and the multi stakeholders in the different projects initiated by the Block Panchayath. Special gratitude to the beneficiaries of the different schemes for sparing their valuable time for the sake of this study.

Prof. K.N. Hailal, Member, Kerala State Planning Board has been instrumental in motivating us to analytically examine the activities of the Nedumangad Block Panchayath and we place on record our due respect and regards to him. Prof. Harilal has been guiding the Block Panchayath in designing and implementing its innovative schemes and has been relentlessly providing his expertise in decentralised governance and development. We would like to place on record our deepest gratitude to him for this effort and also for valuable time he spent for reading the book and writing the foreword.

The academic environment provided by the University of Kerala to its faculty members to engage in research and extension need to be recorded with gratitude. Particular thanks to Prof. V.P. Mahadevan Pillai, Hon'ble Vice Chancellor and Dr. S. Nazeeb, Research Convenor of the Syndicate for inspiring us to pursue action research and outreach activities. Gratitude also to Dr. Prasad A.K., Dr. Abdul Salim, Dr. V. Anitha, Mr. Siddik Rabiyath, Dr. S.R. Sheeja and Dr. Christabell P.J., faculty members of the Department of Economics. Adv.Babujan, Finance Convenor of Syndicate needs to be specially mentioned for always providing constructive landscape for linking university departments to society and economy.

The contributions of our friends, particularly Anupama Augustine and Arya Devi who did the proof reading is recorded with immense gratitude. Finally, thanks are due to our family members who have always stood with us during all our academic endeavours.

Dr. Manju S. Nair

Dr. Saisree K.G.

Vijayasree R.M.

Chapter - I

Introduction

Decentralization as a multidimensional process, acts as a countervailing force in modern times of restrained resource base and burgeoning distributive spectrum, helping people access the benefits of regime change, enabling them to enhance their livelihood (Falleti, 2005). Evidence across the globe regarding the incorporation of decentralised governance in policies and legislations provides testimony to the increasing recognition of the ostentatious merits of decentralisation by national economies. The 73rd and 74th amendments of Indian constitution in the year 1992, that envisaged a new domain of Panchayath Raj Institutions, is such a reform on Indian policy making and governance, that lays out a three-tier administrative structure, at Village, Block and District levels. However, legislative reforms solely cannot suffice the strengthening of decentralized governance that is complex and intrinsic (Eaton et.al, 2011). It requires the structure and functioning of decentralized governing institutions to follow the tenets of good governance with active people's participation and effective resource management; articulating the needs of community, especially the weaker and marginal sections; thereby enabling local civic bodies to become vehicles of social transformation. (Oommen,1984).

The state of Kerala, being the second state in India to adopt the constitutional change is a relevant example of effective decentralisation (Thomas, 2016). Kerala followed a big bang approach to decentralisation, by passing the Panchayati Raj Act, 1994 with a new Panchayati Raj system covering three tiers, namely, Grama Panchayath (lower tier), Block Panchayath (intermediate tier) and District Panchayath(upper tier) and each of these tiers were empowered with an expanded array of functions, functionaries and funds; allowing them to act as units of local self-governance. The powers, duties and functions of the Grama Panchayaths are listed in schedule III of the Kerala Panchayathi Raj (KPR) Act, the Block Panchayaths in schedule IV and those of the District Panchayaths in schedule V of the Act. (basically derived from section 166, 172, and 173 respectively of the KPR Act). The Act also defines the roles and responsibilities of the three-tier Panchayathi Raj System, without transcending boundaries between each tier. The schedules regarding responsibilities were further modified by Act 13 with effect from 24th March 1999.

Redundancy Arguments regarding the relevance of Intermediate Tier

The Kerala State Legislature has defined the role of intermediate tier, the Block Panchayaths in the decentralised planning and development process through Schedule 4 of the Kerala Panchayat Raj Act 1999. The specified role is to enable the Block Panchayaths in building linkages with both the Gram Panchayaths below and the District Panchayats above and to prevent the Block Panchayaths from overstepping into the functions of the Gram Panchayaths. The functions of the Block Panchayath are grouped as (a) General functions and (b) Sector-wise functions. The general functions reflect the rationale of state legislature in creating a Block Panchayath, whereas the sectoral functions suit specific development requirements. The general functions of Block Panchayath are to:

(1) utilise governmental and non-governmental technical expertise at block level;

(2) provide technical assistance to Gram Panchayaths; and

(3) prepare schemes taking into consideration the schemes of Grama Panchayaths in order to avoid duplication and to provide backward, and forward linkages.

These three guidelines generally provide the base for working of the Block Panchayath. The specific sectoral functions assigned to the Block Panchayaths are indicated under Schedule 4 (b), ranging from agriculture to calamity relief and co-operatives. The major institutions, posts and responsibilities transferred to Block Panchayaths are given in tables 1.1 & 1.2.

Table 1.1: Institutions and posts transferred to Block Panchayaths

1.	Agriculture	One post of assistant director and auxiliary Posts
2.	Industries	One post of industries extension officer
3.	Rural Development	The post of Block Development Officer andconnected posts
4.	Social Welfare	Care homes, old age homes ofrespective Places
5.	SC Development	Pre-metric hostels of the respective places,the post of Block Extension Officer
6.	ST Development	Tribal Extension Officer
7.	Health Services	Taluk Hospitals
8.	Health Department (ISM)/Homeopathy	Block level Primary Health Centre/Community Health Centre

Source: Prakash et al. (2013)

Table 1.2: Responsibilities transferred to Block Panchayaths

Agriculture	Farmers' training for the programme simple mented at the village level/Arrangements of agricultural inputs required for schemes at the village level/Conduct of agricultural exhibitions. Integrated water shed managements in water sheds that fall in Block Panchayath area/ Mobilization of agriculturalcredit/Sericulture etc.
Animal Husbandry	Running of maternity policlinics and regional artificial insemination centres/Provision of specialty services in animal husbandry/Conduct of cattle poultry shows/Minor irrigation/All lift irrigation schemes and minor irrigation schemes covering more than one Village Panchayath.
Minor Irrigation	All lift irrigation schemes and minor irrigation schemes covering more than one village panchayath.
Fisheries	Development of traditional landing centres.
Small Scale Industries	Setting up of mini industrial estate/ Promotion of industries withInvestment limit of one third of SSIs/Self-employment schemes in industrial sectors.
Housing	Popularization of low-cost housing/Promotion of housing co-operative societies.

(Contd...)

Electricity& Energy	Promotion of non-conventional energy sources.
Education	Management of industrial training institutes
Public Works	Construction and maintenance of village roads covering more than one village panchayat/Construction of buildings for institutions transferred.
Public Health & Sanitation	Management of community health centres and taluk hospitals within the Block Panchayat area in all systems of medicines.
SocialWelfare	Management of Integrated Child Development Scheme
Poverty Alleviation	Planning and implementation of employment assurance schemes in co-ordination with the Village Panchayaths/ Skill up gradation of the poor for self-employment / wage employment for people below poverty line.
SC/STDevelopment	Management of pre-metric hostels /Promoting scheduled castesand scheduled tribes co-operatives.
Co- operatives	Organisation of co-operatives within the jurisdiction of Block Panchayaths/ Payment of government grants and subsidies within the jurisdiction.

Source: Prakash et al. (2013)

Although specific guidelines are given regarding the roles and responsibilities of the Block Panchayaths, the Block Panchayath level administration in Kerala has faced staunch criticism in the light of overlapping strategies and schemes and block as a mandatory intermediate tier was itself considered redundant in the state by experts. "There was a predominance of beneficiary and service sector schemes and a tendency to replicate schemes which otherwise could have been implemented by Gram Panchayaths. The role of Block Panchayath envisaged as an intermediate level Panchayath and as a facilitator is rarely reflected in the Block Panchayath projects" (GoK, 2009). Several reasons are attributed to this argument.

Firstly, most Block Panchayaths focused their domain on social service sector schemes and productive sector attained less attention, in spite of the fact that Schedule 4 (b) of the Panchayath Raj Act assigns duties with regard to agriculture, animal husbandry, milk production, small scale industries and energy to the intermediate tier. This is distressing as the Block Panchayaths have more funds and autonomy to influence the larger productive sector, whereas social services and allied schemes can be effortlessly coordinated at village level. This made the activities of Block Panchayaths lesser varied in comparison with that of Grama Panchayaths.

Secondly, Block Panchayaths in the state lack dynamism in (a) adequate exposure to the need and potential of development through convergence and coordination of expertise of various department functionaries, (b) area specific allocations of centre and (c) grass root level access of lower tiers. "The elected members of the Block Panchayath are not aware of the Central Government assisted development programmes being implemented through the Block Development Office. The Block Panchayath programmes do not integrate their development activities with the Community Development programmes which are implemented and monitored by the Rural Development Department" (GoK, 2009).

Finally, the block, conceived as an intermediate level between the district and village do not adequately facilitate forward and backward linkages in formulation and implementation of schemes and strategies. Schedule 4(a) of the Panchayath Raj Act reiterates the role of Block Panchayath in facilitating linkages relating to the utilization of technical expertise, making available technical assistance to Gram Panchayaths. However, the advantages envisaged to be reaped by Block Panchayath as an intermediary between Grama Panchayats and District Panchayat has not happened and over the years Block level administration has been observed by expert committees to be a challenging one for a small state like Kerala, where the chances of overlapping functions and policy heads between block and village level administration are high (Vijayanand, 2009; Menon, 2016). The relatively large size of Grama Panchayaths and the relatively small area of District Panchayaths makes it difficult to invest the Block Panchayaths with a meaningful set of functions (Vijayanand S M, 2009). Also an understanding of the financial devolution to the Block Panchayaths shows that the funds at the disposal of the Block Panchayaths is not sufficient to meet their functions, to quote Prakash, B.A.(2013) "regarding the financial situation of the local bodies of Kerala, the extent of financial devolution to Grama Panchayaths has been relatively high when compared to District Panchayaths and Block Panchayath".

Statement of Purpose

It is observed from the literature critiquing the relevance of an intermediate tier in a decentralised governance system, that the functioning of Block Panchayaths fail at a point where the statutory characteristics of the level are breached for convenience in execution and where the functional role is rarely distinguished from that of other tiers, particularly Grama Panchayaths. However, evidence on instances of inadequacies in the functioning of Block Panchayaths cannot lead to a generalised judgement on the redundancy of an intermediate tier. This is because, contrary to the general picture of dismal performance of Block Panchayaths in Kerala, there is the case of a particular Block Panchayath – Nedumangad Block Panchayath in Thiruvananthapuram district – effectively performing not only its general and specific functions, but also adopting innovative and sustainable interventions, which has led it to bag the DeenDayal Upadhyay Panchayath Shaktheekaran Puraskar (award for the best Block Panchayat in India, instituted by the Central Government) and Swaraj Trophy (award for the best Block Panchayth in Kerala, instituted by the State Government), consecutively for 2017-18, 2018-19 and 2019-20. Nedumangad Block Panchayath stands out as an illustration with replicable merits, because it has proved that the specified general and sectoral functions assigned to a Block Panchayath can be performed effectively with an optimal mix of good governance, resource management and people's participation. Further, the activities and schemes adopted by the Panchayath are in tune with sustainability interests, with a long-term achievable target of strengthening resource base, management of natural resources and consequently creating sustainable livelihood, under the larger purview of environmental governance. The present study identifies the case of Nedumangad Block Panchayath as a success model; tracing and analysing its developmental initiatives and delineating the factors responsible for the same; providing evidence to substantiate the relevance of an intermediary tier in the decentralised governance regime in the state of Kerala.

Profile of Nedumangad Block Panchayath

Nedumangad Block located at the East-West part of Thiruvananthapuram district came into existence in 1954 and in 1994, the Nedumangad Block Panchayth was institutionalised; consisting of

Panavur, Anad, Aruvikkara, Vembayam and Karakulam Gram Panchayaths. (Local Body Code O 0106000). The detailed demographic profile of Nedumangad Block Panchayath is shown in table 1.3. As per 2011 census, the Block Panchayath has a population of 1,76,478 with 45,754 households within a geographical area of 123.51 sq.km and population density of 1192. The literacy rate of the Block is 90.15 (with 94.2 for males and 86.24 for females) which is lower than the state average of 94 per cent (96.11 per cent for males and 92.07 per cent for females).

Table 1.3: Demographic Profile of Nedumangad Block

Population	147296
Male	72573
Female	74723
Population Density	1192
Sex Ratio	1030
Literacy Rate	90.15
Literacy Rate (Male)	94.2
Literacy Rate (Female)	86.24

Source: Census, 2011.

Figure 1.1 Map of Nedumangad Block Panchayath

Nedumangad Block Panchayath coordinates and conducts all developmental activities and interventions under the broad vision of "SAMRUDHI" (Sustainable Agricultural Management and Rural Development Initiative). Nearly forty model projects have been implemented since 2015 of which the popular ones are 'Jaivagramam', 'Anganwadi Jaivagramam', 'Killiyar Mission', 'Vallam Nira', 'Ksheerasamridi', 'Agri-business', 'Kalagramam' etc. The Block is also recognised as the first Block Panchayath in the state which obtained ISO certificate in 2015 and is declared as the first Geo Informatic Block Panchayath in India with the support of GIS Planning, coordination, monitoring and management in 2017. Consequently, in recognition to the sustained efforts, Nedumangad Block Panchayath received many prestigious awards including the DeenDayal Upadhyay Panchayath Sasakthikaran Puraskar for its outstanding efforts and initiatives consecutively during 2017-18, 2018-19 and 2019-20,Swaraj Trophy during 2017-18 and 2018-19, Prathibha Puraskar for excellence in performance of Block Panchayath President during 2017-18, award for best performance innovative approach in health sector from Ayush International Conclave during 2017-18 and for the best ATMA Group from Department of Agriculture, Government of Kerala in 2016-17.

Design of the Study

The objective of the study is to trace and analyse the developmental initiatives of Nedumangad Block Panchayat and to delineate the factors responsible for its successful performance. For this, a conceptual and practical framework is developed with focus on statutory functions of the Block Panchayath and adherence to the principles of good environmental governance.. Details of conceptual and practical framework of the study along with the methodology adopted and brief documentation of sector specific developmental initiatives of the Block is provided below.

Conceptual Framework

Figure 1.2 Conceptual Framework for Analysing Factors enabling the successful functioning of Block Panchayath

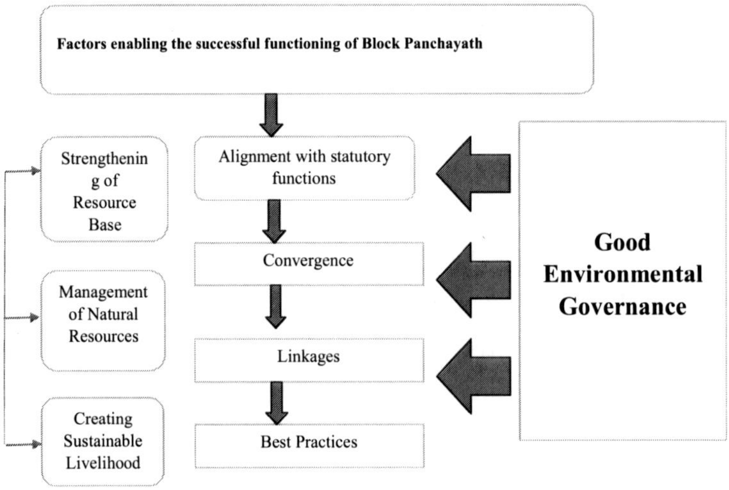

Nedumangad Block Panchayath should judiciously use its capacity and functions by statute, facilitating a well-balanced convergence of various State departments, central/state schemes and adjacent tiers. This fosters adequate linkages, aiding best practices in strengthening of resource base, management of natural resources and livelihood creation; under the larger lens of Good Environmental Governance. Environmental governance is a notion about how societies deal with environmental problems; the interactions between formal and informal institutions and actors in society, and their influence on the identification and framing of environmental problems; and the ways in which environmental issues reach the political agenda, policy formulation and implementation, at both global and local levels (UNCDF, 2005). Environmental governance is based on the following premises:

(a) Sustainable development initiatives occur at the local level;

(b) Good governance is based on the identification of individuals and institutions that should be empowered to make decisions about natural resources and their management;

(c) Local governance structures must be strengthened in order to fully assume environmental roles;

(d) Communities should not only share the benefits arising from the use of natural resources, but also participate in decisions regarding their management;

(e) Local stakeholders need to be individually and collectively empowered in order to adequately address sustainability issues.

Local self-governance institutions at the intermediate level can intervene on reshaping the mode of functioning of existing system, by facilitating guidance and support with a futuristic local natural resources management orientation. If so, the unique natural resource base of the local economy can be adequately tapped, strengthened and managed for creating sustainable livelihood through proper environmental governance.

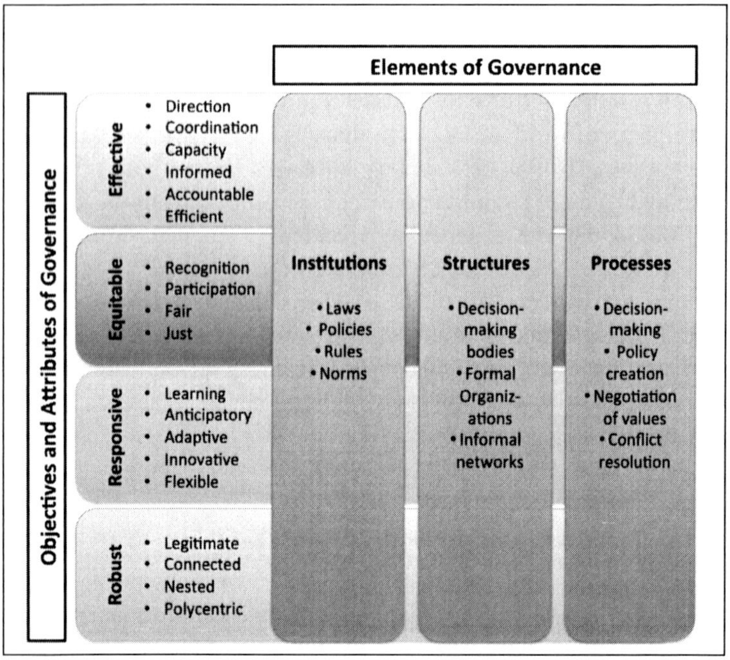

Bennett, N.J. & Satterfield, T. (2018). Environmental governance: A practical framework to guide design, evalution, and analysis. Conservation Letters. https://onlinelibrary.wiley.com/doi/abs/10.1111/conl.12600

Figure: 1.3: A practical Framework for Environmental governance

The aim of environmental governance, in particular is to manage individual behaviours or collective actions in pursuance of public environmental goods and related societal outcomes (Armitage et al., 2012; Termeer, Dewulf, & Van Lieshout, 2010). It helps to understand how decisions related to the environment are made and whether resultant policies and processes lead to environmentally and socially sustainable outcomes and an analysis of environmental governance focuses on the capacity, functioning, and performance of the institutional, structural, and procedural elements of governance. Structures, institutions and processes in general determines how and for whom decisions are made, whether, how and what actions are taken and by whom and to what effect (Graham et al., 2003; Lockwood et al., 2010) under the environmental governance framework, which further determines the ways and means by which individual and collective actions are managed.

The various elements of environmental governance should encompass the attributes of robustness, responsiveness, equity and effectiveness; determining the practicability and sustainability of a good environmental governance strategy. Effectiveness in the environmental governance context implies the ability of a system to direct, coordinate and in its capacity as a change agent, to be informed, accountable and efficient. Clear direction is provided through precision in the articulation of vision, goals, aims, and the establishment of distinct boundaries on action and scope (Graham et al., 2003; Lockwood et al., 2010; Wyborn, 2015b). Second, to achieve the objective of being socially equitable, environmental governance should engage decision-making processes and produce socioeconomic outcomes that might be characterized as: inclusive, participatory, fair, and just. Equitable environmental governance begins with policies and processes that recognize, respect, and are inclusive of the perspectives, knowledge systems, values, cultures, and rights of diverse stakeholders (Borrini-Feyerabend et al., 2015; Lockwood et al., 2010; McDermott, Mahanty, &Schreckenberg, 2013), including the views of groups who are often marginalized (e.g., women, indigenous peoples, or minority groups) or vulnerable (e.g., impoverished communities). Effective participation requires context and scale-specific spaces, processes, and structures to enable inclusion, representation, and engagement of stakeholder groups in collective decision-making processes (Lockwood, 2010; Reed, 2008). This facilitates the sharing of power, democratically debated decisions, maintenance of dignity, and the creation of representative plans and actions. Power- and benefit-sharing mechanisms can help ensure that the socioeconomic benefits and burdens of conservation and environmental management that are distributed in a fair manner, and that rights and responsibilities are shared and assigned commensurate to circumstances (Bennett, Teh et al., 2017; Pascual et al., 2014; Zafra-Calvo et al., 2017). Finally, equitable governance is safeguarded when laws and policies are present to protect local rights and tenure, ensure that consent is freely given, and groups have access to justice to defend against incursions.

Third, responsiveness ensures that environmental governance is adaptable both to changing environmental and social conditions and to diverse contexts. Responsive environmental governance arrangements exemplify: learning, anticipation, adaptability, innovation, and flexibility. Finally, good environmental governance system need be robust functioning institutions – persisting over time, maintaining performance, and coping with perturbations and crises. Robust environmental governance institutions are legitimate, connected, nested, and polycentric. Evaluations and deliberations guided by the framework shall also support efforts to design and improve the capacity, functioning, and performance of governance systems (Bennett and Satterfield, 2018).

The practical framework that the study adopts is applied to better understand environmental governance in decentralised social contexts, for diverse issues and at a range of scales, since it is discerned that the activities of Nedumangad Block Panchayath is based on the premise of good environmental governance and fits within the stated framework and sustains the growth prospects with a long-term vision. The report on one hand enquires upon how Nedumangad Block Panchayath performs the general and sectoral functions of Block as visioned by the statute and on the other hand analyses the dynamics of good environmental governance that promotes adaptability and capacity utilisation which is embedded in the various innovative schemes and projects that it undertakes.

To understand the activities and strategies of Nedumangad Block Panchayath; the research team made observational visits to the Block and had several rounds of detailed reflective discussions with President, elected representatives, officials and beneficiaries of the various schemes. Indepthinterviews were conducted with implementing officers including Block Development Officer, agriculture officer, medical officer and extension officers. Focus Group Discussions were conducted to assess the activities of different committees and other community-based organisations and to elicit views, opinions, information and suggestions from the stakeholders. The bool is based on the evidences we have from these sources and also from the documented policy initiatives and interventions.

Sectoral specific interventions of Nedumangad Block: Integrating Statutory Functions and Environmental Governance

Nedumangad Block Panchayath through its dynamic schemes, sequential projects, innovations and determination in implementation; express distinct prioritisation of the needs of the locale, across time scale. The period analysed is characterised by optimal combinations of interventions at Block level; integrating tiers at district and village level, and effective utilisation of technical expertise of State departments. Such an integrative approach has enabled Nedumangad Block Panchayath to add a new dimension to environmental governance through management, strengthening and reiterating sustainability of resources. The section gives a broad outline of the various sector specific initiatives adopted by Nedumangad Block Panchayath over the last four years, under the conceptual framework integrating statutory functions of the block and the concept of environmental governance.

At the level of implementation; environmental governance is a socio-ecological and participatory sustainable development process; targeting enhanced livelihood status of the rural poor. For this, enabling convergence among various departments and activities of adjacent tiers were conceived as an important method for effective intervention by Nedumangad Block Panchayath; facilitating the creation and execution of innovative programmes that subsequently improve the socio-economic conditions and guarantee inclusive participation of the target group in developmental activities. This was materialised through elements of good environmental governance under decentralised system, integrating dynamic institutions, effective decision-making structures and pragmatic sequence of execution; facilitating a coordinated, judicious and adaptable mechanism. The thrust areas identified for integrated intervention by Nedumangad Block Panchayath were Agriculture, Public health, Public works, Entrepreneurship and Social welfare. Innovations were channelized through a spectrum of schemes and projects for promoting:

(a) Women centric organic agriculture and animal husbandry practices,
(b) Rural industries through agri- business incubation centre,
(c) Natural resources restoration through rejuvenation of Killi river
(d) Infrastructural development through Resource Recovery Facility
(e) Universalised public health care services

Women centric organic agriculture and animal husbandry practices

Nedumangad Block Panchayath identifies sustainability in terms of livelihood, resilience and adaptability, under the broader framework of environmental governance, particularly Agro-Environmental Governance, through active involvement of women and children as primary agents of change and creating efficient institutions, structures and processes. Initiatives were formulated for ensuring adaptive capacity of local governance for socio-ecological resilience through integrated farming practices. Consequently, the Block established the "Jaivakrishi Pariseelana Sevana Kendram", a 'Model Integrated Farming with Organic Agriculture Training Centre', along with several subset schemes to the larger SAMRUDHI vision during 2015-18, including an organic nursery, Fallow less Bio village (Tharishurahitha Jaivagramam), Organic garden for kindergartens across the block (Anganwadi Jaivagramam) and other projects for provision of self-sufficiency in food and nutrition at household level (*VallamNira*). As the block popularized integrated agricultural practices; animal husbandry was a complementary sector that developed and subsequently became one of the major areas of interventions by the Block Panchayath, targeting seeping of benefits through women. For this, Ksheerasamrudi Dairy farms were visualised and implemented to work in association with MGNREGS and Dairy Development Department.

Rural industrialisation through agri- business incubation centre

Agro-Environmental Governance in its broader sense encompasses rural industrialization, which further diversifies production possibilities in agriculture and fosters community development strategies through entrepreneurship. Following the lines, Nedumangad Block Panchayath started an Agri-Business Incubation Centre, for creating an entrepreneurial platform for rural farmers and upcoming entrepreneurs. The initiative aims to reduce the post-harvest losses of the villages and also provides attractive and cost-effective processing systems for agricultural commodities. Training facilities were also provided with focus to trigger the minds of entrepreneurs to embark into food business.

Natural resources restoration through rejuvenation of Killi river

Pollution and soil erosion along the banks of the Killi river were serious problems being faced by five villages under Nedumangad Block. Killiyar Mission, a convergence mission mode initiative was undertaken to build pollution and encroachment free embankments for preventing soil erosion and floods. Block Panchayath authorities and Haritha Kerala Mission in convergence with the MGNREGA planned and executed this mission spreading over the jurisdiction of five Panchayaths of Nedumangad Block Panchayath. Implementation of this mission has increased the level of the embankment and reduced the threat of floods for along the 22 kilometres of the river and its 33 rivulets.

Infrastructural development through Resource Recovery Facility

One of the recent paradigm shifts in waste management globally is the change in approach from 'managing waste' to 'managing resources'. This should entail the possibility of a sustainable circular economy wherein recycling is incorporated into the production-consumption dual. Resource Recovery Facilities are one such progressive waste management system adhering to the sustainability and resonance principles of Environmental governance, wherein a Resource Recovery Centre is envisioned as a space provided with necessary infrastructure, machinery, tools and human power to sort, clean and store non-biodegradable discards from primarily sorted municipal waste and made available for production or consumption purposes. Nedumangad Block Panchayath is an instance of a civic cluster outperforming in this front, in convergence with the Grama Panchayaths, Shuchithwa Mission and other agencies.

Universalised public health care services

Health care is distinguished by the diversity of services that are covered by the term. Care may involve prevention or treatment of disease; treatment may be for acute or chronic problems; health problems may be exclusively individual or have collective dimensions, or they may be specific to particular groups (for example, children or women); and, increasingly, health care includes attention to broader aspects of well-being (N. Singh, 2008). In this varied requirements and targets of health and well-being, it is essential that accountability at local level need be assured through delegation of powers. Block level interventions are essential for its ability to penetrate locally and coordinate various state level health schemes and policies. Nedumangad Block Panchayath considers interventions through community development as the primary path for health sector development and introduced four health programmes - "Jyothir Gamaya Balya"-improving the health status of children between the age group of 3 months to 3 years; "Jyothir Gamaya Kaumara"-improving mental and physical health of adolescents through counselling given to parents, teachers and children between 13 years to 17 years in higher secondary schools; "Raksha"- for giving awareness about the cancer detection and referral system, and "Amrutham Gamaya Jeevana"- aimed to raise physical and mental wellbeing of elderly in the villages through physical activity, Yoga. All these programmes were conducted by Nedumangad Block

Panchayath in coordination with various government schemes and departments, ensuring local accountability and convergence.

Thus, Nedumangad Block Panchayath was able to identify and implement innovative developmental projects and interventions, integrating the elements of good environmental governance, made possible under the decentralised governance structure, with the broader view of sustainable development. To elaborate, the Panchayath was successful in identifying the challenges in each sector, the need and path for intervention and the sequential actions in terms of projects and schemes were designed and tailor made to address the gaps identified. Following chapters details the sector wise actions and specific interventions adopted by the Block Panchayat which provides a testimony that Block Panchayath has its own importance in the decentralised planning scenario.

Chapter - II

Agriculture and Animal Husbandry

Brief

Nedumangad Block Panchayath conceives sustainability in terms of livelihood, resilience and adaptability. In this composition, utilizing the adaptive capacity of local governance for socio-ecological resilience through integrated farming practices was identified as the strategy and women and children were associated as the primary agents of change. The Block Panchayath established a "*Jaivakrishi Pariseelana Sevana Kendram*", a 'Model Integrated Farm with Organic Agriculture with several subset schemes to the larger SAMRUDHI vision during 2015-19, including an Organic nursery, Fallow less Bio village (*Tharishurahitha Jaivagramam*), Organic garden for kindergartens across the block (*Anganwadi Jaivagramam*) and other projects for self-sufficiency at household level (*Vallam Nira*) were also formulated. These initiatives have transformed nearly 400 hectares of waste land to cultivable land, under the jurisdiction of block, featuring a productivity of 6000 tonnes of vegetables and fruits; 12.5 tonnes of flowers, providing employment to 5000 labourers per year since implementation. Since the block popularized integrated agricultural practices; animal husbandry was a complementary sector that was focussed, which subsequently became one of the major areas of interventions by the Block Panchayath, targeting seeping of benefits through women. Co-ordinating MGNREGS and Dairy Development Department, the Block provided guidance for Ksheerasamithi Dairy farms which has now emerged as a replicable initiative.

Challenge and Need for Intervention

Socio-ecological resilience has become a very important concept in sustainable development. This is based on the understanding that there is an urgent need for both planning and management that can give social, economic and environmental benefits to the people which leads to sustainable development (Srinivasrao et al. 2016). The capability of the food systems to deal with social, economic and environmental change, especially in the value chain process (Vroegindewey and Hodbod 2018) also becomes important in this context. However, in praxis there is no ideal way to solve the problems associated with food systems at once, owing to the fact that agriculture inherently is intertwined with socio-economical and agro-ecological contexts in which the community exists. Here an Agri-Environmental Governance approach is needed, (Agri-environmental governance (AEG) works here as an encompassing concept to understand how environmental issues are addressed within the food system by a set of diverse actors of the public and/or private sectors (Forney, 2016), wherein organic farming is identified as an effective multi layered strategy to integrate resilience (FAO/WHO, 2001; IFOAM, 2002). Also, though the approach of resilience is diverse; the notion of adaptive capacity or adaptability of actors in a system to influence resilience (Folke et.al, 2010) is imperative and requires a series of well-developed and structured planning procedures. The intricate nature of desired outcomes in this background stresses the role of decentralized government structures in disseminating knowledge to the farmers; establishing land patterns and creating sensible policies. Further decentralized governance can aid developing organic markets and related infrastructure; providing help to the farmers to maintain an organic transition for the health and environment of the society. Over the period under consideration of the report, Nedumangad Block Panchayath has followed target specific interventions, and Agriculture has been a thrust area. The Block has strategized sustainable interventions through integrated farming practices under the broad spectrum of organic interventions. Also, animal husbandry was developed to complement the sustainability targets, focusing on the fact that the local economy is historically dependent on animal rearing and bases its subsistence on it. The Block thus recognised the relevance of animal rearing, especially the dairy sector along with organic agriculture in alleviating poverty and unemployment, thus fitting into the larger picture of Agri-Environmental Governance.

Action

It is discerned that the Block has focused on productive sectors, particularly agriculture, animal husbandry and milk production in consonance with the duties assigned to a Block Panchayath as per Schedule 4 (b) of the Panchayath Raj Act. The pattern of various interventions made by the Block Panchayath in Agriculture and dairy sector is an evidence to the fact that the Block has followed the three important premises of Agri-Environmental Governance.

(a) Sustainable development initiatives occur at the local level

(b) Good governance is based on the identification of individuals and institutions that should be empowered to make decisions about natural resources and their management, and

(c) Local stakeholders are individually and collectively empowered in order to adequately address sustainability issues.

Based on this premise, following are the major interventions made by the Block Panchayath.

Bio village or Jaivagramam

The first plan was to set a model to sustainable farming, by starting organic agriculture in the land owned by Block Panchayath and developing it as an agriculture hub, by which slowly the whole village could be transformed. Three acres of barren land owned by the Block Panchayath was brought under organic cultivation, the Block Committee members and officials of the block shared the initial cost amount of Rs. 4 lakhs for clearing the land and cultivated five items of vegetables viz, ladies finger, cowpea, bitter gourd, snake guard and cucumber. All Block members, including the President, their family members and block officials, and some likeminded enthusiasts provided the labour activities required for farming. The ward members were given the responsibility to nurture the farmland at the initial stage and thereafter the responsibility to maintain the farm was entrusted to workers within the village. The farmland now follows an integrated farming system where poly house, barn, aqua culture, floriculture and butterfly garden exist in proximity to take advantage of interaction benefits. The produced vegetables are sold to local households and nearest markets; and profit is returned to the block itself. As of now, the Bio village gives permanent income to seventeen workers, and about seventy workers are getting temporary employment. The programme is running successfully with a profit margin of more than rupees three lakhs per year.

Fallow less Bio village

After the success of *Jaivagramam* initiative, the Block Panchayath decided to convert the wasteland available under its jurisdiction for cultivation purposes and the farmers, local people and owners of the private land supported this initiative which resulted in the conversion of 400 acres of cultivable waste land into organically cultivated one. At first, the Block decided to initiate cultivation in ten hectares of leased private land, but the local residents agreed to offer their land to Block Panchayath without rent for a period of three years. From cultivation in these fallow areas, a profit of Rs. 3.73 lakhs was earned by the Block during the year 2017-18, out of which an amount of 1.73 lakhs was credited to the own fund of the Block.

Also, the Block Panchayath in association with Grama Panchayaths decided to bring all cultivable waste/barren land under cultivation in a phased manner. As part of this project it was decided to form forty cluster groups, each with five to twenty members. In the first phase, the scheme was implemented in three Grama Panchayaths of Karakulam, Panavoor and Aruvikkara. From these Panchayaths, one ward each was selected for implementation. Waste/barren lands were identified by the representatives of Block Panchayath, selected group representatives, Grama Panchayath and Agricultural Officers of concerned Krishi Bhavans from each ward. They identified ten ha of waste land from the Karayalathukonam ward of Karakulam Panchayath, 11ha from Meenilam ward of Panavoor Panchayath and 9.5 ha from Kalathukal ward of Aruvikkara Panchayath. The team converted the land into one that became suitable for cultivation with the inputs from agriculture department and soil conservation department; and cultivated around 110 metric tons of vegetables, tubers, banana, papaya etc from these areas.

Organic farming Training Centre

On the basis of the successful experience from the organic farming of vegetables in the premises of the Block Office, the Block Panchayath initiated a project to develop the culture of organic farming among farmers in all the five Grama Panchayaths of the Block. With this aim, the Committee decided to establish a Training Centre for organic cultivation to impart training to farmers and to develop the attitude to foster low cost organic farming systems suitable for regional conditions. Therefore, a training centre named *Jaivakrishi Pariseelana Sevana Kendram* was registered as per the Travancore – Cochin Charitable Societies Act 1955 and the centre started functioning from November 2016. Around 400 organic farmer groups were formed in five Grama Panchayaths and these groups were registered with the centre. Members of these groups were given training for different types of organic/integrated farming methods, with a view to sensitize the importance of sustainable farming practices. Further organic farming knowledge dissemination was adopted through distribution of booklets, elaborating methods and techniques of organic farming. This centre is showcased as a model of integrated farming practices, demonstrating interrelated and interdependent nature of farming activities and principles of productive utilization of farm wastes and fuller utilization of manpower with available resources. The underlying spirit behind the model were triggered by Agri-Environmental governance principles of economic sustainability through organic farming; rejuvenation of the productivity of soil; maintenance of agroecological equilibrium; and control of insects, pests, diseases and weeds through different methods of agro-ecological engineering such as floriculture, fish culture, and livestock raising.

The Block level nursery

For popularising organic farming, the centre got sanction from the Agriculture Department for starting an organic nursery for the production and distribution of quality seedlings. The Department also provided financial assistance of Rs. seven lakhs for the nursery with provision to construct poly house under the Vegetable Development Programme during the financial year 2016-17. The poly house helped in large scale production of organic seedlings which were distributed for the regional and state level agricultural programmes such as "Vallam Nira", "Haritha Keralam", etc. Seedlings of vegetables, sesbane (agastya), ginger, turmeric, Moringa oleifera (muringa), neem, plantain and flowering plants were the most prominent seed varieties produced under the scheme.

Organic Farming through grow bags

One of the major intend of environmental governance is to motivate local people to participate and become agents of change and Agri-Environmental practices starts with generation of interests among local stakeholders wherein Nedumangad Block identified consumer households as focal point in order to support and share the responsibility of increased agricultural production. The Block Panchayath launched a scheme to popularise 'grow bag cultivation' during 2016-17, mainly intended to those who do not possess land and for those interested, through organic farming. A total of 1000 units (beneficiary groups), with 200 from each Panchayaths, were formed and were supplied with 25 grow bags, costing Rs. 80 to Rs. 200 per unit. The total cost of the scheme was Rs. 20 lakhs, in which the Block Panchayath allotted an amount of Rs. 10 lakhs from own fund during 2016-17, each Grama Panchayath shared Rs. 1 lakh and the beneficiaries' contribution was Rs. 5 lakhs (each unit had to pay Rs. 500). Those beneficiaries who could not raise their own fund, were given the possibility to avail interest free loans from State Cooperative Banks. Organic grow bags with vegetable seedlings including chilli, ladies finger, tomatoes and brinjal were distributed in the first phase and indigenous medicinal/flowering plants were supplied in the second phase.

VallamNira Project

Another important project launched by the Block Panchayath is Vallam Nira during 2016-17, aimed to achieve self-sufficiency in the production of vegetables especially during festival seasons including Onam and Christmas. This was implemented through Self Help Groups of the five Gram Panchayaths. Households with at least ten cents of land were encouraged to cultivate vegetables through organic method. The seeds, seedlings and manure were distributed through the Jaiva Krishi Pariseelana Sevana Kendram of the Block Panchayath. Prior to the implementation of the scheme 4200 SHGs (Kudumbasree), each comprising 5 to 20 members were formed. For the implementation of the project, SHGs organised JaivaSabhas in 98 wards, participated by 28000 villagers, out of which 21000 were Kudumbasree members. Thus, Nedumangad Block Panchayath became the first Local Government in the state which had started to organize organic jaivasabhas for vegetable and flower cultivation. Around 1500 monitors from each unit were entrusted to coordinate and supervise the implementation of the scheme. Four types of medicinal seedlings such as sesbane (agastya), malabar tamarind, neem and sweet neem (curry tree) and three types of flowing plants such as vadamalli, marigold and jasmine were distributed through this scheme. In the first phase these seedlings were distributed to the beneficiaries by Community Development Societies (CDS), Area Development Societies (ADS), and elected members of Block and Grama Panchayaths. In the second phase these seedlings were distributed to the wards which were convened by JaivaSabhas. The scheme is being monitored and reviewed regularly by the Block Committee with the help of officers of Agriculture Department. The surplus vegetables and flowers from households were collected by these monitors and given to the shops/stalls for sales. Apart from making the villages self-sufficient in vegetables and flowers, these activities also helped in creating employment opportunities to the rural poor, especially women.

Anganwadi Bio village

Even though Kerala has impressive human development indices and an effective system for child health related services, the latest National Family Health Survey (NFHS-4) reveals that one third of children in the age group 6 months to 6 years are anaemic. Twenty percent of children below 5 years are stunted and 16 percent are wasted.

As such, apart from the normal intervention, specific programmes should be planned and promoted at micro level to improve the nutritional state of children. It is in this context that the Block Panchayath initiated a programme named "Anganwadi Organic Village" during 2016, to improve the nutrition status of children who were enrolled in the Anganwadi centres. The specific objectives of the programme were the following:

- Reduce the prevalence of anaemia among children in the age group 6 months to 6 years.
- Include safe and harmless vegetables in the daily diet of the children.
- Increase the interest of children and parents towards natural foods.
- Promote the culture of organic farming by avoiding toxic chemical fertilizers and pesticides.
- Create awareness among children regarding organic farming and to ensure community participation for the smooth functioning of Anganwadi centres.

Initially, a direction was given to the Anganwadi Centres to identify one cent of land within its premises or nearby places for growing vegetables. In the next stage, the department provided seeds and organic manure for cultivation and the officials in charge, monitored the activities, so as to ensure scientific planting and nurturing of seedlings. The harvested vegetables were to be used for preparing morning, mid-day, and afternoon meals for children and it is observed that all centres produced the required organic vegetables throughout the year. The scheme is implemented in 164 Anganavadi centres, 2 bud schools for differently-abled kids and 20 lower primary schools. This also facilitated a Horticulture Therapy (HT- The motto of HT is "towards ability from disability") focusing on people –plant connection or engagement of a person in gardening and plant-based activities, being very important for the physical, mental and social well-being in the care of children and aged people. For each Anganwadi Centre, a welfare committee was formed to monitor the activities, of which the ward member of the local government is the chairman and anganwadi worker is the convenor. The project became successful because of the inter-departmental convergence and public participation

Actions targeting Dairy Sector

Women centric expansion of dairy farms were conceptualized by the Block Panchayath as a prominent livelihood enhancement strategy on the ground that earnings by women further filter down as funds for children's schooling, investments in small agriculture, purchase of additional livestock and asset accumulation. This has a multiplier effect to the primary efforts and the actions taken by the Block in this front is based on a sequential approach.

Initially, a pilot convergence project under MGNREGA was initiated with the line department (Dairy Development Department) by the Block Panchayath during 2016-17. The objective of this initiative was to ensure sustainable livelihood to the selected women groups. This particular project focused on providing ten milch cows to each women group consisting of ten targeted beneficiaries. The beneficiary groups were selected on the basis of certain criteria, such that at least two or three members should have knowledge about cattle rearing or should have at least one milch cow. The average cost of a milchcow was estimated to be around Rs. 40,000, with the beneficiary contribution being 50 percent and the Government subsidy for the remaining 50 percent. It was also felt that many women groups may not have ready cash to contribute their share of 50 percent to avail of the benefits of this initiative. To deal with this problem, beneficiaries were linked with banks through the District Cooperative Banks or Nationalised Banks, in consultation with the Dairy Development Department. This helped the beneficiaries to avail loans for buying cows and each group got Rs. 2 lakh as bank loan and Rs. 2 lakh as subsidiary amount from government. The government's share in the form of subsidy for purchase of the milch cows was provided through funds available under the Dairy Development Department and Mahatma Gandhi National Rural Employment Guarantee Scheme (MGNREGS).

The Block Panchayath's other contribution to this initiative include giving assistance for infrastructure facilities including construction of cow shed and provision of subsidies for cow mats, milking machines, fodder cultivation etc.The construction of shelters for cows was to be taken up by beneficiary's contribution or by loan amount. After the construction of cowsheds and installation of infrastructure facilities, it was the responsibility of the dairy development officer to supervise the selected beneficiary area and to recommend the sanctioning of subsidies for the selected beneficiaries. The beneficiaries were also encouraged to develop fodder in their own land with funds from MGNREGA and construction of shelters for cows was taken up under MGNREGA. The selection of the beneficiary families was done through the gramasabhas and each beneficiary was given permission to buy milch cow at their own interest but not from their own region. This scheme was availed by eleven groups with 110 beneficiaries in 2016-17. In the second phase during 2017- 18; considering the viability, availability and productivity of this initiative, Block decided to expand the reach of this initiative region wise, optimising the output with ten groups of five members and two groups of six members, the total number of beneficiaries beingsixty two. The average cost of a milch cow was estimated to be around Rs. 50,000, with the beneficiary contribution being 50 percent and the Government subsidy for the remaining 50 percent. This helped the beneficiaries avail loans for buying the cows and each group got Rs. 2.5 lakh as bank loan and Rs. 2.5 lakh as subsidy amount from government. With the strengthening of Ksheerasamrudhi dairy farms; the average income of the selected women self-help groups has increased to Rs. 2.5 lakh per annum.

Marketing and diversified value creation were strategized later, so as to strengthen the economic viability of the scheme. As part of this, the members of the groups sold their products to the nearby milk co-operative society. They also earn an average of Rs. 50000 per year through the sale of calves, cow dung and curd.

Discussion

The schemes and initiatives of the Nedumangad Block Panchayath in the agricultural front were formulated, by adapting to the statutory functions and by embedding the philosophy of environmental governance.

Firstly, it is observed that in contrast to the most other Block Panchayaths in the state; Nedumangad has rightfully acknowledged the conceptual distinction of the intermediary tier in the decentralised system. Nedumangad Block Panchayath stands out in its policy peculiarities, focusing on productive sectors, primarily agriculture and animal husbandry, as against other Block Panchayaths focusing on service sectors. This is significant as Gram Panchayaths and its functionaries have limited role to play as individual units in facilitating changes in the productive sectors. The schemes like FallowlessBiovillage, VallamNira etc, exemplify the strategy of Nedumangad Block Panchayath to trigger development through investment in productive sectors, which is much larger to the purview of Gram Panchayaths.

Secondly, it is observed that all the efforts on revamping productivity ensured sufficient backward and forward linkages, indicating how efficiently Nedumangad Block Panchayath carries out its constitutionally delegated functions. Regarding the bottom end, the activities of the Block were so formulated as to coordinate various Gram Panchayaths under its jurisdiction. The project Vallam Nira (encouraging consumer households to cultivate vegetables organically), which was implemented coordinating SHGs of five Gram Panchayaths under the Bock's purview, Jaivasabhas that were formed with authorities of Gram Panchayaths as monitors and the Jaivakrishi Pariseelana Kendram; initiated to develop the culture of organic farming functioning with the sufficient support and participation from all the five Gram Panchayaths of the Block are instances of grassroot level linkages. Linkages at the top end is observed wherein the Block Panchayath efficiently implements the state schemes and policies by drawing from the expertise of state departments and its functionaries. Funds from various schemes were appropriately channelized and agriculture development was viewed as a path to rural self-sufficiency and independence.

Thirdly, in the cultivation front, the Block Panchayath acts as a facilitator connecting various stakeholders adopting a "learning by doing" approach, whereby modification, selection, conflict resolution, discussions, as well as experimentation with new ideas for the management and sustaining of agriculture was ensured. The success of the Block in popularizing organic practices are found to be rooted in the philosophy in administration, political dexterity in implementation and popular participation; all being the elements of good environmental governance, that makes the system responsive to the needs, by being adaptive, innovative and participatory – a learned approach. Barren lands, the significant yet less addressed concern of every locality is judiciously put to cultivation by the Block and there has been cooperation and coordination in leasing out the uncultivable land, free of cost. Cultivation prospects were widened through Kudumbashree initiatives, bringing in value addition and innovation. Along with expanding production prospects, the Block Panchayath has also adopted strategies to disseminate farm knowledge, reinforcing the sustainability of initiatives. The relevance of organic practices were dispersed through indigenous farmers and experts. Educational institutions and the Panchayath functionary themselves were identified as trusted source of dissemination of right practices. This strategy has enabled the Block Panchayath to embark on effectiveness in service delivery through directing, coordinating and creating accountable and efficient system.

Fourthly, Nedumangad Block Panchayath has conceptualised sustainability in a composite manner. Animal rearing and dairy, the sectors that had longitudinally been an anchoring force in alleviating poverty, was discovered as a potential sector for creating rippled outcome. Under the ambit of various schemes, all the Gram Panchayaths under Nedumangad block jurisdiction were harmonized. Immediate results were evident in improvement in the total milk production of the locality (creating self-sufficiency in consumption) and enhancing the economic return of the beneficiaries. Further, resilience at household level was reinforced by institutionalizing organic farming system through training Centre and organic nursery. The vision of the Block and the ambitious prospects of diversification were demonstrated with model farms. A key distinction of the Block's initiatives were that they were self-sufficient holistically. Simultaneously, while a model farm was created and organic practices were popularized, the functionaries also made sure that the inputs also are sustainable and at best organic.

Finally, care was exercised in identification of target groups and beneficiaries, particularly women and children. Women centric activities mainly through Kudumbashrees enable a multi layered intervention, for the economic independence of women is vital and triggers social development. Alongside, the spirit of sustainable livelihood is expected to regenerate over time as seeds are well planted in young minds through various policies incorporating educational institutions and Anganwadis as beneficiaries.

Altogether, the Block Panchayath on the one hand was successful in performing its general functions, using technical expertise, creating backward and forward linkages and made visible impacts through the coordination and convergence of line departments. On the other hand, capitalising on the institutions, structures and processes that the decentralised governance facilitates; Nedumangad Block Panchayath has created a platform to make the whole process of environmental governance and the consequent development; robust, responsive, equitable and effective.

Chapter - III

Rural Industrialisation through Agri-business incubation centre

Brief

Rural industrialization has a difficult task of inducing change in a rural milieu and should focus on technology and skill development in the context of either the problem-oriented, sectoral or community development strategies (FAO, 1981). Therefore, the nature and pattern of decentralized interventions in rural industrialisation should adopt to the specific capabilities of each locale. Considering the established platform of agricultural activities in the Nedumangad Block Panchayath; enhancing agricultural entrepreneurship through Agri-Business Incubation Centers forms an ideal expanse. In 2017-18; Nedumangad Block Panchayat started an Agri-Business Incubation Centre, for creating an entrepreneurial platform for rural farmers and upcoming entrepreneurs. The initiative aims to reduce the post-harvest losses of the villages and also provides attractive and cost-effective processing systems for agricultural commodities, particularly fruits, vegetables, plantain, tapioca, coconut, spices and rice. The focus of training is to trigger the minds of entrepreneurs to embark into food business. The centre conducts yearly training/ workshop on entrepreneurship development programme on food processing to budding entrepreneurs who are seeking ideas for their business.

Challenge and Need for Intervention

The process of decentralization and the conception of the functions of an intermediate tier includes active involvement with the productive sectors of the local economy, predominantly the agriculture sector. However, sustainability in localised agricultural contexts is a complex concern and should coordinate the multiple aspects of economic viability particular to the place, judicious use of environmental resources that is widely available and social coherence at grassroots. This has an objective of narrowing the gap between food needs and localised food production. The existing prospects of the sector is mainly dampened by post-harvest loss and non-availability of trained labour. In this circumstance, the Block Panchayath identifies women as the primary catalysts of change and aims to increase participation of rural entrepreneurs in agri-businesses by making systematic investments to enhance participation and productivity, aiming to create and sustain agriculture-based livelihoods through Agri-business units in the locale.

Agri-business incubation is defined as a process which focuses on nurturing innovative early-stage enterprises that have high growth potential to become competitive agribusinesses by serving, adding value or linking to farm producers. The agribusiness incubation process typically provides shared facilities and equipment; business development, market access, and technology assessment services; financial services; and mentoring and networking (Dev, 2011)). Food processing incubators, a variant of Agribusiness Incubation, have the objective of stimulating entrepreneurism and technological innovation; intended to provide requirements of food sector, including necessary facilities for labelling, traceability, familiarity with food industry regulations, designing of packaging, the setting of expiry dates and adapting to market needs. Nedumangad Block strategizes involvement with rural industries through the broader SAMRUDHI project, bringing together sustainable rural livelihood and self-sufficiency by capitalising the resource base in Agriculture through agro-based industries.

Action

The project SAMRUDI envisages an innovative idea of establishing an Agri- Business Incubation centre to impart training to the farmers and upcoming entrepreneurs and how to convert the locally available raw products into finished agricultural products. Accordingly, machinery have been installed in the incubation centre and in the first phase 60 selected entrepreneurs have benefitted from free training for a period of 20 days. As a beginning, basic primary machinery and equipment were purchased and placed in the incubation centre for the value addition of jack fruit, banana, pineapple, coconut, vegetables etc. The Agri-business centre contains boiler and kettle, multipurpose and multifuel drier, Acoconut de sheller, disintegrator, fruit pulper, fruit miller, pulverizer, freezer, packing machine, band sealer, water purifier, stove, vessels, CCTV camera, bio gas plant and other essential equipment. In the first phase Centre for Management Development was assigned to impart training. The trained entrepreneurs were further provided with the possibility of utilising the facilities of the centre by paying a small user fee. Handholding services were provided for entrepreneurs who based their economic activities on value added products from locally mobilised crops. This was facilitated under the aegis of industries extension officer of the block and financial institutions (provision of loans). Also, sixteen of the trained entrepreneurs were selected to work in the Agri Incubation centre in Mundela, Aruvikkara Gram Panchayath, where the Block Panchayath makes value added products.

The Centre was formally inaugurated after testing for its efficiency on 29th January 2020 and has trained 100 entrepreneurs since 2018, in two stages to make value-added products from local produce. The Block Panchayath aims to encourage micro cluster of agri-based entrepreneurs, by establishing a mutually beneficial ecosystem of farmers and agri-entrepreneurs, wherein the farmers would supply the raw materials to the entrepreneurs. The centre will further provide marketing services to the products made at the incubation centre and the same would be sold under the Block Panchayath's 'Samrudhi' project. The cost incurred so far for the project is 18.5 lakh for machinery and another `6.9 lakh for training and affiliated projects.

Discussion

Nedumangad Block Panchayath identifies productive sectors, particularly agriculture as the pivot and industrialization and capacity building is envisioned through diversification at value addition level. The activities of the Block in this front is an expansion of environmental governance practices with a big picture of sustainability.

Firstly, appropriate structures are elementary in creating micro clusters of entrepreneurship to a locality where the concept itself is novel. The Block Panchayath has facilitated the creation of appropriate structure by facilitating a training centre and machinery for those who are interested. With the systematic training, people are empowered with an ability to start with their own production units. Also, the centre provides handholding services and facility to use machinery at a nominal fee to users, enabling optimal use of equipment and other facilities.

Secondly, interventions need to be effective and robust when addressing sustainability in a broader purview. The local produce is effectively put to use, reducing wastage due to post harvest loss to the minimum. Post-harvest loss is often reported as an import issue in agriculture, due to lack of adequate infrastructure in storing of products and value addition. The Agri business incubation Centre, initiated by the Nedumangad Block Panchayath ensures that local agricultural produce is effectively put to use through value addition.

Finally, the rural agro-based industries which will be developed within the ambit of Agri business incubation would encourage farmers and entrepreneurs to take risk-averse business initiatives. Also in addition to training, continuity in agro-industrial activities was assured by the Block as it acts as a facilitator for further expansion of each initiative by providing guidance in availing subsidies from various departments and agencies like Women Development Corporation, Small Scale Industries Development Corporation (SIDCO), Khadi and Village Industries Board and so on under various schemes. The entrepreneurs were also assisted by Industrial Extension Officer (IEO) on the provision of careful support or guidance during the learning process, availing licences and clearances from various departments like Local Self Government, Kerala Electricity Board, and Kerala Pollution Control Board for technical support. The Centre also facilitates obtaining Food Safety and Standards Authority of India (FSSAI) licences and by virtue of this license the entrepreneur can produce quality food products individually or by utilising the incubation centre. Here again the role of Block Panchayath as a link between various Government departments and their schemes is evident, wherein the line departments are coordinated and the broader schemes at state and other levels are properly channelized.

Chapter - IV

Killiyar Mission

Brief

Pollution and soil erosion near the banks of the Killi River were serious problems faced by five villages of Nedumangad Block. Killiyar Mission, a convergence mission mode initiative was undertaken to build pollution and encroachment free embankments for preventing soil erosion and floods. Block Panchayath authorities and Haritha Kerala Mission in convergence with the MGNREGA planned and executed this mission spread over the jurisdiction of five grama panchayats of Nedumangad Block Panchayath. Structures and institutions formed and the process that was adopted during the implementation of the Mission under the environmental governance framework determined the ways and means by which individual and collective actions were managed. Implementation of this mission has increased the level of the embankment and reduced the threat of floods for along the 22 kilometres of river and its 33 rivulets.

Challenge and Need for Intervention

The restoration, conservation, and management of rivers or watersheds are becoming one of the major thrusts in resource management projects across all countries, as conflicts on shared water resources are increasing and ecosystem of watersheds tends to become fragile owing to agricultural, industrial and urban domestic usage. The problem of degraded watershed and its management is a complex and multi-dimensional one and its sustainable development can only be made possible through participatory watershed development approach. Apparently fostering human resources, creating awareness, cultivating skills and capabilities in youth to work and manage in watershed development, and nurturing water resources on a sustainable basis becomes important. The scenario of decentralised governance, if used properly can provide ample setting for successful management of the aforesaid through adopting people centred or auxiliary approaches with use of balanced inputs and partnership of agencies having common interest resulting in collective action. In this context, Nedumangad Block Panchayath runs the participatory watershed management program, by adopting scientific and unique planning and implementation under the environmental governance frame work to manage individual behaviours and collective actions in pursuance water shed management and related societal outcomes.

Action

Killiyar originates from Karinchathanmoola in Panavoor Gram Panchayath of Nedumangadu Taluk in Thiruvananthapuram District, the capital city of Kerala. The river, with an average width between 19m to 20m, pass through different habitats such as rural, semi-urban areas and agricultural landscape for about 32 km and finally joins the Karamana River at Kalladimukham near Thiruvallom. The Killi River flows through five Panchayaths around twenty-two kilometres within the Nedumangad Block Panchayat. Of these, it covers five kilometres through Panavoor and Anad Panchayaths, one kilometre through the Aruvikkara Panchayath, eight kilometres through the Karakulam Panchayath and eight kilometres through Nedumangad Municipality.

Studies have documented the fact that the river gets polluted while flowing, a major reason being dumbing of garbage including left-over from slaughter houses and fish markets, opening of sewage pipeline to the river, open defecation by local people, bathing of cattle and laundering. In addition, encroachment of riverside for cultivation and construction and sand mining activities disrupts natural flow of water with harmful effects on quality of water and biodiversity in the area.

Killiyar Mission, initiated by the Block Panchayath, Nedumangad is a participatory project for rejuvenating river Killiyar in which local self-government authorities, people's representatives, various government departments and local people joined hands successfully to clean the river to ensure its free flow through its entire course. The mission covered twenty-two kilometres area from Ottakkombu-Karinchajathimula-Tirthankara to Vazhayila and the whole stretch having an average width of 19 m was cleaned. The Mission not only created an ecological value but added a social and economic value since the people in the area heavily relied on the river for meeting their primary needs, agricultural activities and for fishing. These activities hither to was being threatened by the unprecedented amount of waste dumped into the river. The mission aimed at sustainable management of Killiyar river and its environment and water ecosystem through decentralised and participatory development processes as evidenced by the objectives of the programme given below,

- Creating awareness among local people about the significance of Killiyar and the extend of pollution effected in the river ecosystem by conducting 'Puzhayarivu' program.
- Organizing a one-time event (One day cleaning programme) with the support of all stakeholders to clean the river and its tributaries to ensure regular flow and to maintain water level in the river during the whole year.
- Ending the encroachment on the river basin by adopting regulatory measures
- Eliminating sources of water pollution with the help of nearby landowners and institutions
- Ensuring mindful use of water resource to meet the needs (drinking and irrigation) of local people.
- Guaranteeing protection of river side and catchment area by planting trees and beautification along with rejuvenation of local water bodies including wells

The project was carried out in several stages by synergising various stakeholders including the District, Block, Gram Panchayaths, Municipal Council, Forest Department, Water Resources Department, Sanitation Mission, Health Department, Agriculture Department and

Revenue Department. It turned out to be an innovative and dynamic environmental management programme for the Block Panchayath, coordinating general public and government, with various objectives, managing different elements and integrating multiple financial sources.

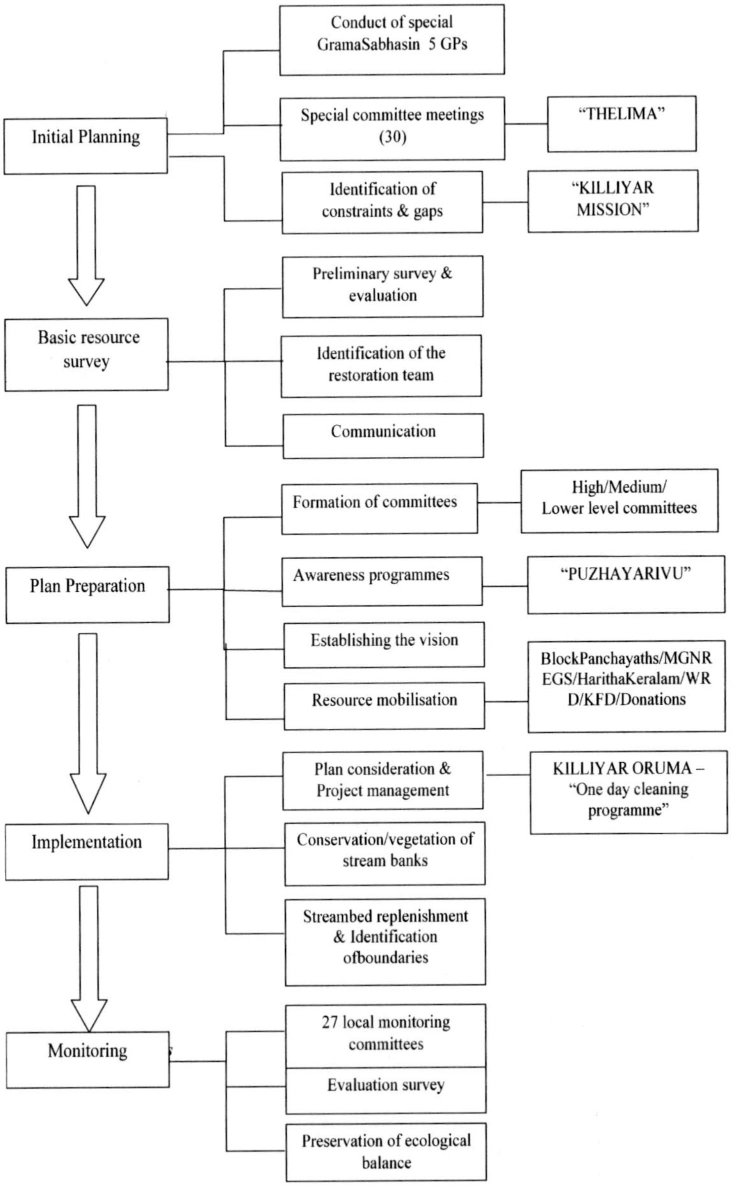

Source: Authors construct.

Figure 4.1: Initial Planning

Killiyar Mission- Phase 1

The first phase of Killiyar Mission consists of five stages namely; Initial Planning, Basic Resource Survey, Plan Preparation, Implementation and Monitoring, each described below.

Initial Planning

The first step towards initial planning consisted of efforts towards community mobilisation to initiate collective action. This stage of watershed development program involved various discussions held for analysing the problems associated with Killiyar by conducting local level meetings and initiating discussions in gramasabhas. The authorities of Block Panchayath named it as "Thelima" since the activities in this stage were directed towards assessing the existing situation and planning the mission with support of all stakeholders.

Basic Resource Survey

The main purpose of second stage was to identify the processes that have contributed towards pollution of the river and the possible areas of intervention, which was completed through a preliminary survey. At this stage the available man power for the program was identified with the support of ward members in each Panchayath. With a vision to create public opinion on the matter and attract people and professionals from various spectrum of stakeholders, a call for restoration was done by the Block Panchayath. The aim was to create a joint vision of Killiyar mission and discuss the feasibility of the mission, so as to identify the hurdles and plan accordingly. Support was received from all government departments, civil society actors and local people and the strength of decentralisation was seen in this unique endeavour of deepening democracy where public opinion raised in Gram Sabhas and meetings at different tiers of government acted as the base for formulation of the program which was implemented with the help of various government authorities. At this stage the Block Panchayat sought support from various government agencies/departments such as Suchitwa Mission, Irrigation Department, Forest Department, Revenue Department and a consensus was reached with regard to a joint action by all stakeholders.

Plan Preparation

A working model for watershed management program was developed at this stage. The Block Panchayath and the Urban Council decided to organize a centralized Killiyar Mission Convention which was to be led by Nedumangad Block Panchayath. The Patron Committee was constituted, comprising of Ministers, MPs, MLAs, District Panchayath President, District Collector and Municipal Chairman. A Killiyar Mission Committee was formed comprising a Chairman and Convener. Special Conventions and Mission Committees were constituted at Gram Panchayaths and Urban Councils. The committees were divided into higher level committee, mid level committee and local level committee. Regional Killiyar Mission Committees were also set up at major Centers from Tirthankara to Vazhayila.

Implementation / Plan Execution

The one-day cleaning program- 'KilliarOruma' made the actual difference in the area and it showed how common lands can be protected through mobilisation and collective action at the grass root level. A meeting was organised by Nedumangad Block Panchayath and Haritha Kerala Mission. The Killiyar Mission Committees of all levels joined together and conducted this mass meeting, which was held on 14th April 2018 and was called locally 'KilliyarOruma'. In the one-day long cleaning campaign thirty two thousand people cleaned the 22 km of river and its 31canals/channels, materialising the theme of the programme "Killiyar will flow calmly" (Killiyar Ozhukum Swasthamayi). The cleaning campaign aimed at removing pollutants gathered over the years and ensured that the river will flow peacefully or freely in future.

Monitoring

Killiyar Mission has been envisaged as a program to foster rural development process, via strengthening the governmental structures and by capitalising labour force at stake, through a participatory approach where the demand for development comes from public opinion. At present 27local/regional committees serve as monitoring committees. As part of its ongoing work, the municipality and the village panchayat have closed more than 1,000 drainage pipes which helped in makingthe riveras a source of clean water.

Killiyar Mission- Phase 2

After the successful conclusion of the first phase of Killiyar Mission, a detailed report was prepared by the Irrigation Department, with an estimate of 8.45 crores for the second phase beginning from February2020, that will include constructing check dams, parks for recreation, fencing and pathways, planned at reclaimed land. For the purpose, proper demarcation of the river boundaries will be completed in the grama panchayats of Karakulam, Aruvikkara, Anad, and Panavur and the Nedumangad municipality. On 14th of February, 2020 the second phase of Killiyar Mission flagged off with a collective participation close to 25,000 people, led by local self-government bodies in each respective region where the river passes through. By 2020-end, the Block panchayath hopes to declare Killiyar as 'Kara Kaviyaatha Killiyar' (a river that does not overflow) and the demarcation of river boundaries in the Karakulam panchayat (totalling 16 km on both banks) is expected to be completed by June 10.This will cover two km (both banks) at Aruvikkara, six km at Anad and Panavur, and 16 km in the municipality area. Apart from the Killiyar Mission, Jalasangamam and PradeshikaKilliyarSangamam will also be organised to ensure continuity and sustainability of the programme with public participation.

Discussion

Efficiency and sustainability of watershed development programs is determined by the quality of institutional structures created during the project period, and interactions among them and with other relevant agencies active in the vicinity (Sreedevi T.K., 2008). Killiyar Mission is a unique experimentation of watershed development in Kerala as the programme achieved success within a short span of time and the institutional arrangements and interactions among different institutional structures that happened over the period, ensembles both the properties of proper environmental governance and the advantages of collective action, made possible through democratic decentralisation.

Firstly, the ad hoc organisational and institutional arrangements established during the mission period in the form of primary stakeholder organisations and institutions are the most important part of arrangement that made the program a success. The local level committees constituted by including the members of MGNREGA, Ayyankali Urban Employment Guarantee scheme and local people acted as the primary stakeholders who were both executers and beneficiaries of the scheme. On the one hand, the Block Panchayat succeeded in ensuring monetary benefits to the primary stakeholders who are attached to employment guarantee schemes for taking part in the mission, and at the same time all the local people were given awareness by conducting, Puzhayarivu, the awareness program and thus the need and social value attached to the mission was popularised. This double pronged strategy adopted by the Block Panchayat ensured whole hearted support from primary stakeholders, and their apprehensions were resolved through dialoguing. Also, monitoring committees with local people as members were constituted for looking into the encroachments and to prevent the sources of pollution, which helped in creating a sense of ownership about the program among local people. Two principles of environmental governance were adhered to in the process; (a) the actions were based on the identification of individuals and institutions that should be empowered to make decisions about natural resources and their management (b) local stakeholders need to be individually and collectively empowered in order to adequately address sustainability issues.

Secondly, an important aspect of the program was the diverse institutional support structures ranging from Mid-Level Committees to High level Committees including people's representatives, technicians Kudumbasree members, social activists, students and nature lovers. These committees were directly involved in providing technical support and in issuing administrative clearances. Here the interactions among different institutional structures is noteworthy, these interactions being both structural and functional.

Thirdly, the scientific approach followed, by conducting a study on the current status of pollution and submitting the reports to various departments and then by leading a grass root level movement demanding a watershed program ensured the smooth functioning of the program. The Block Panchayat succeeded in making their idea of watershed development as a product of common consensus and the stakeholders who participated in the program felt ownership of the program and this helped in settling the opinion differences among various stakeholders. The Killiyar Mission is thereby both an intervention and outreach initiative abiding to the principles of good environmental governance, wherein the aim of the mission was primarily to manage individual behaviours or collective actions in pursuance of public environmental goods and related societal outcomes (Armitage et al., 2012; Termeer, Dewulf, & Van Lieshout, 2010). People were sensitized on how decisions related to the environment are made and whether resultant policies and processes lead to environmentally and socially sustainable outcomes and an analysis of environmental governance focuses on the capacity, functioning, and performance of the institutional, structural, and procedural elements of governance.

Finally, in most of the watershed development programs, post project sustainability is a major issue since the institutional arrangements cease functioning once the project period is completed. However, Killiyar Mission, a joint initiative of the Haritha Keralam Mission, the district planning committee, Jalasree Mission, the Nedumangad municipality, and grama panchayats in the region; has overcome this problem since the primary stakeholder committees has a more political nature and they continue their work since it includes social activists, people's representatives, labours and local people. The monitoring committee is active during the second phase of the mission and priority is given to the removal of encroachments near river basins. Another major initiative in the phase is proper demarcation of the river boundaries that have been completed in the Grama panchayats of Karakulam, Aruvikkara, Anad, and Panavoor and the Nedumangad municipality with the aim to stop further encroachments. Similarly, measures to protect the river banks by planting trees is going on with the intention to sustain the efforts. In addition, Trivandrum Corporation has announced and initiated 'Killiyar City Mission' to clean the rest of the river that flows through its jurisdiction.

Chapter - V

Resource Recovery Facility

Brief

One of the recent paradigm shifts in waste management globally was the change in approach from 'managing waste' to 'managing resources'. This should entail the possibility of a circular economy wherein recycling is incorporated into the production-consumption dual. Resource Recovery Facilities are one such progressive waste management systems, wherein a Resource Recovery Centre is envisioned as a space provided with necessary infrastructure, machinery, tools and human power to sort, clean and store non-biodegradable discards from primarily sorted municipal waste and made available for production or consumption purposes (http://sanitation.kerala.gov.in/). The recyclable waste will be sorted and channelized for recycling while the non-recyclable plastics are shredded and used for road tarring. Nedumangad Block Panchayath in convergence with the Gram Panchayaths, Shuchitwa Mission, and other agencies has initiated the RRF within the Block Panchayath premises, which intends a comprehensive system for plastic waste management, coordinating efforts from collection of wastes to final disposal.

Challenges and Need for Intervention

Successful governance should encompass well designed policies for resource management, highlighting possibilities for a 'circular economy' (Otoo and Dreschel, 2018). The concept of Circular Economy intends a shift from 'take, make, dispose' to incorporating recycling to the production-consumption cycle and offers multiple benefits including ecological economics, green growth and sustainable development. Also in the context of resource scarce countries, it is more than opportune to argue for a circular metabolism, as increasingly promoted in many developed nations, where waste segregation and recycling contribute to overall system resilience (UNEP, 2017) and the values of green growth, i.e. an economy without degrading the environment (Otoo and Dreschel, 2018). However, analysing the context of India in general and Kerala in particular, the green development strategies which are in its infancy lack a working model that propel stakeholders to act on the basis of social and environmental concerns, and consider these as concrete bottom lines in their policy decisions. This is where Resource Recovery Facilities assume significance in progressive waste management system. The Suchitwa Mission by Kerala State proposes establishment of Resource Recovery Centres at cluster/Block level. The Resource Recovery Centres will be a space provided with necessary infrastructure, machinery, tools and human power to sort, clean and store non-biodegradable discards from primarily sorted municipal waste and made available for production or consumption purposes. The recyclable waste will be sorted and channelized for recycling while the non-recyclable plastics are shredded and used for road tarring. Nedumanagad Block Panchayath is a civic body that has effectively perceived the concept and has implemented it appropriately.

Action

As part of resource management activities, Nedumangad Block Panchayath during 2018-19 has realised Resource Recovery Facility- a major scheme for progressive waste management, with the coordinated efforts of Grama panchayaths and other agencies. It is envisaged that the effective functioning of RRF in the block would enable a participatory collection and material recovery, thereby realising a plastic free block, aligning with using plastic waste in a most environment friendly manner. Further, the RRF would propel dissemination of awareness and would create gainful employment opportunities. The Block Panchayath runs the RRF center in association with the Clean Kerala Company, Haritha Karma Sena, Grama Panchayaths and Suchitwa Mission, with a total fund of 27 lakh from Suchitwa Mission and 34.68 lakh from plan fund.

Taking into consideration the apprehensions of natives on the health consequences of the processing plant, RRF was constructed within the premises of the Block Panchayath, after scientifically examining the desirability of the same. Solid waste from five Gram Panchayaths are collected and segregated at MCF Centers and RRF unit, wherein recyclable plastic waste are pressed and others are shredded, which are then collected by the Green Kerala Company with a monthly target of 5000kg. Shredded plastic is further used for road construction locally. As on 30.09.2019, a total of 20059.01 kg non-renewable plastic were shredded out of which 8059.01kg were sold.

Discussion

A thorough examination of a waste management system should consider factors from the point of waste collection to final disposal (Dubanowitz,2000) and Resource Recovery Facilities is a unique way forward, which facilitates transforming waste materials into useable resources. Recycling here represents a method of managing solid waste while reducing pollution, conserving energy, creating jobs and building more competitive manufacturing industries. The initiatives of the Nedumangad Block are welcoming in this pursuit.

Firstly, it need be mentioned that the initiative of the Block was despite of the fact that waste management is not a direct responsibility of the Block Panchayath. However, Nedumangad Block Panchayath has ratified the conception of RRF, with a view on waste management being integrated and inseparable cause and need for the development of several other sectors. It is noteworthy that Nedumangad Block Panchayath has played a role of facilitator and provider in the initiative, rather than supporting Gram Panchayaths through fund allocation. In this context, RRF scheme that is conceptualised by converging Gram Panchayaths and other agencies is a replicable instance of a local body, specifically an intermediary tier performing functions with a holistic view.

Secondly, RRF is a viable economic model of sustainable resource management, optimising economic benefits and welfaristic intentions. RRF scheme once operationalized in full capacity, would be a source generating own fund for the Block Panchayath. The Clean Kerala company has set a monthly target of 5000 kg treated plastic from the center and the price after covering for the labour cost and operating expenses of the center is the own fund of the Block Panchayath. However, this estimated benefit will be realised only once the center starts functioning, utilising its full capacity.

Further on economic front, currently the scheme provides larger skill development and employment opportunities for the residents, with further plan to expand the prospects of the same.

Thirdly, the activities of RRF fall in direct correspondence to the wider goals of Environmental governance that sustainable development initiatives occur at the local level and Good governance is based on the identification of individuals and institutions that should be empowered to make decisions about natural resources and their management. Through well thought strategizing of waste disposal across the Block, Nedumangad Block Panchayath strengthens the structures in order to fully assume environmental roles. Taking into consideration the apprehensions of the local residents on the waste management plants, the block has constructed RRF centre within its premises, giving confidence to public and being accountable.

Finally, orienting to the effectiveness and equality attributes of environmental governance, it is observed that RRF functions transparently and the recent social audit agrees with this.

Resource value is at best maximised by extending the useful life of products through resale, repair, and refurbishment, implying a transformational promise to a circular economy. These opportunities demand major shifts in governance practice and implementation, incorporating incremental changes alongside readily achievable gains. The RRF scheme and its functioning at Nedumangad Block Panchayath is a judicious mix of both outcomes.

Chapter - VI

Public Health

Brief

Health care is distinguished by the diversity of services that are covered by the term. Care may involve prevention or treatment of disease; treatment may be for acute or chronic problems; health problems may be exclusively individual or have collective dimensions, or they may be specific to particular groups (for example, children or women); and, increasingly, health care includes attention to broader aspects of well-being (N. Singh, 2008). With decentralisation, the Local Self Governments got the possibility to navigate through the multiple challenges faced in the health care sector and to provide necessary policy solutions through a community-based approach, with focus on preventive care along with curative care. Nedumangad Block Panchayath considers interventions through community development as the primary path and introduced four health programmes - "Jyothir Gamaya Balya"-improving the health status of children between the age group of 3 months to 3 years; "Jyothir Gamaya Kaumara" - improving mental and physical health of adolescents through counselling given to parents, teachers and children between 13 years to 17 years in higher secondary schools; "Raksha"- for giving awareness regarding cancer detection and referral system, and "AmruthamGamayaJeevana"- aimed to raise physical and mental wellbeing of elderly in the villages through "Yoga". All these programmes were conducted by Nedumangad Block Panchayath in coordination with various government schemes and departments, ensuring local accountability and convergence.

Challenge and Need for Intervention

Health care services in policy lens, moves beyond a focus on individual behaviour towards a wide range of social and environmental interventions, particularly in the context of decentralized service delivery, wherein various stressed groups need to be attended to. Paediatric and adolescent health care is one of the basic issues in policy front, among which malnutrition is both a condition and contributing factor for several other diseases. Identifying the cause and addressing the needs timely is often neglected at governance end and curative treatment is by and large assumed to be sufficient. Negligence in child health can severely influence child development, their educational attainments and their potential to lead productive lives. Geriatric health care is a similar area where preventive treatment, curative medicines and other supporting services should work hand-in-hand. Care should be focused mainly on motivating the elderly to enthusiastically overcome the difficulties associated with ageing and on giving proper care. Along with attending to the needs of vulnerable groups, preventive care of non-communicable diseases is another thrust area where a local body can have pertinent role. Most importantly, for diseases like cancer with an incidence rate of 135.3 per one lakh people in Kerala, disease screening facility at local level is important as individuals themselves rarely initiate a diagnostic check.

The prominent solution for these health care needs is community participation, by providing proper training and awareness programmes to the community. To induce long-term changes in the health of a society, there is a need for continuous improvement in the society's ability to solve various health problems and creation of a healthy environment. This process of transition towards a healthy society is a continuous one where inputs and interventions from local governance becomes very crucial. Innovative services, new programs, and sustainable resources provided through Local Self Governance, can contribute much to improve the health profile of a locality. Nedumangad Block Panchayath has made remarkable contributions in this field by innovative health care schemes, disseminating knowledge related to healthy living and adopting preventive, curative and promotive health care programmes.

Action

Jyothir Gamaya Balya and Jyothirgamaya Kaumara

With an aim to develop a model comprehensive health care project which enables optimum utilization of potentials of Homoeopathy in health care, and effective integration of medical and non-medical components in health care delivery, Nedumangad Block initiated two major projects addressing the health care needs of children and adolescents - Jyothir Gamaya Balya and Jyothirgamaya Kaumara.

The Jyothirgamaya Balya project was implemented as a voluntary pilot project in 2016-17 and the working fund was raised as sponsorship from LSG members, hospital staff and co-operative societies and NGOs. As per this project, a team of Homoeopathic doctors visited 164 Anganavadis and evaluated health status of children and the identified cases were specially evaluated and directed to nearest Dispensary or Taluk Hospitals. Patients with serious diseases were encouraged to follow conventional treatment standards and homoeopathic home remedy kit were also supplied. In the second phase during 2018-19, a team of 77 consisting of doctors, post graduate students, health committee members, political leaders and teachers revisited all the Anganwadis were the scheme was implemented and progress was assessed.

As part of non-medical interventions in health care, the Block Panchayath initiated Jyothirgamaya Kaumara, under which counselling programmes for parents, teachers and adolescents were conducted. The project is organised in association with Kerala State Council for Child Welfare and Aardram Mission during 2018-2019.

The block committee has succeeded in the formation of community group for monitoring these counselling programmes, the members of the group being parents, teachers, political leaders and selected students. The Block organised ten workshops and eight counselling programmes covering all higher secondary and secondary schools under its jurisdiction. The objectives of the workshops were provision of personal assistance to adolescents who were in need, encouragement of positive behaviour, prevention of mental aberrations and promotion of health and wellness. The theme of the workshops mainly focussed on health promotion such as parent-adolescent communication, depression, smoking, sexual health, alcohol & drug use, and risk taking, mental health, violence, physical activity, obesity, nutrition, and social exclusion.

Amrutham Gamaya Jeevana

Nedumangad Block Panchayat has constructively initiated the Amrutham Gamaya Jeevana programme, addressing the medical and non-medical health care needs of elderly in the Block. It is a challenging task for a local body to create an ample atmosphere in which people can age well, maintaining their health and wellbeing for their entire life span. The block conducted homeopathic medical camps for elderly and conducted yoga classes for aiding mental and physical fitness. The programme was visioned in association with government homeopathic hospital, CHC Nedumangad, and Aardram Mission during 2016-17 and 2017-2018.

Raksha

Along with child and elderly health care; the Block has also made significant interventions in early detection of cancer in women. Project Raksha was hence envisioned in association with Regional Cancer Centre (RCC), Thiruvananthapuram during 2017-18 and 2018-2019. The programme focuses mainly on the early detection of cancer and providing awareness to the women in matters of self-detection and preventive care. The doctors from RCC extends the cancer screening facilities to the rural areas through this initiative by organizing screening camps in community health centres (CHC) with the help of block authorities. Screening and awareness camps were attended by 451 women during 2017-18 and 1186 women during 2018-19 with the fund of Rs. 5,00,000 and Rs. 2,00,000 respectively. Individuals attending the camps were screened for oral, breast, cervical and other types of cancers. Women diagnosed to have abnormalities on clinical breast examination were invited to attend RCC for further examination.

In addition to these four health care programmes, the initiatives implemented in the Agriculture sector mainly Jaivagramam, Vallam Nira and Anganwadi Jaivagramam has pertinent role in rooting health care as a life style among the local community.

Discussion

Nedumangad Block Panchayath has introduced four health care programmes collaborating and partnering with various departments such as State Health Department, Kerala State Council for Child Welfare, Regional Cancer Centre-Thiruvananthapuram and Aardram Mission since 2016. The interventions of the block are novel in approach for it brings together the multiple aspects of healthcare delivery, incorporating healthy life style through practicing and promoting organic agriculture, placing emphasis on all systems of medicine and giving special attention to vulnerable communities.

Figure 6.1: Mode of Implementation of Health Care Initiatives by Nedumanagd Block Panchayath

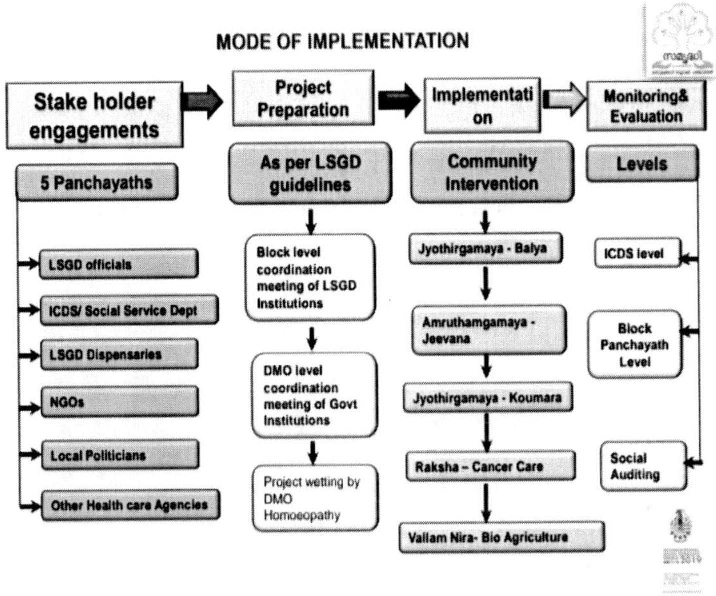

Source: Local Self Governing Leaders Meet, 2019.

Firstly, the Block effectively identifies the health care needs of specific vulnerable groups in the society (children, young adult, women and aged) and gives a holistic care, through a comprehensive health care model which enable optimum utilization of potentials of Homoeopathy in health care and effective integration of AYUSH systems in a health care delivery structure. This enables larger penetration of the benefits of the implemented health care schemes.

Secondly, Nedumangad Block acknowledges in all its schemes and projects that health care is not the responsibility of the individual alone. Instead health is perceived as a collective responsibility. This spirit is embedded in screening and preventive care facilities and regular medical camps initiated by the Block. Most importantly, the patients with notified illness are referred to further treatment and are assisted in all stages.

Thirdly, all the pilot projects are further followed up and regular revisiting of strategies are made. This has helped in effective implementation of various projects and convergence of various departments and schemes is observed.

Finally, the Nedumangad Block panchayath adheres to its underlying vision of one health, whereby the health of soil and health of man is viewed complementary. Organic agriculture is the identified thrust area wherein schemes that empower the local community, especially youth and children in cultivation practices is expected to further yield rippled benefits in healthcare to the community.

Chapter - VII

Successful Decentralisation at Intermediate Level: Delineating the Factors Responsible

The Kerala State legislature has defined the role of intermediate tier, the Block Panchayath in the decentralised governance system, so as to foster a working linkage between the village level and district level administration and delegates functions preventing the Block Panchayaths from overstepping into the functions of other tiers. The statute entrusts the Block level administration to perform its functions by utilising the governmental and non-governmental technical expertise and by effective convergence. In its sector specific roles, the Block level is the starting point of interventions in productive sector. These guiding principles generally provide the base for working of the Block Panchayath. However, the relevance and practicability of an intermediate tier in local governance is questioned by experts and academicians alike. This is in the context of the blocks in general performing functions that overlap with that of adjacent tiers. Also, the functions unique and specific to the block level administration is less performed by most Block Panchayaths in Kerala. In contrast to the general trend, Nedumangad Block Panchayaths has several specific characteristics which make their interventions unique, conceiving the issue of sustainable societal outcomes through a larger perspective of good environmental governance with long term goals. Following provides an examination of the reasons for the effective performance of Nedumangad Block Panchayath.

Firstly, the successful functioning of Nedumanagad Block Panchayath traced during the four year period under consideration is found to be rooted in the administration performing in alignment with the statutory provisions. The block is necessarily an active link between the upper and lower tiers. Regarding the bottom end, the activities of the Block were so formulated as to coordinate various Gram Panchayaths under its jurisdiction. All the initiatives by the block in the various sectors that the study considers is undertaken in

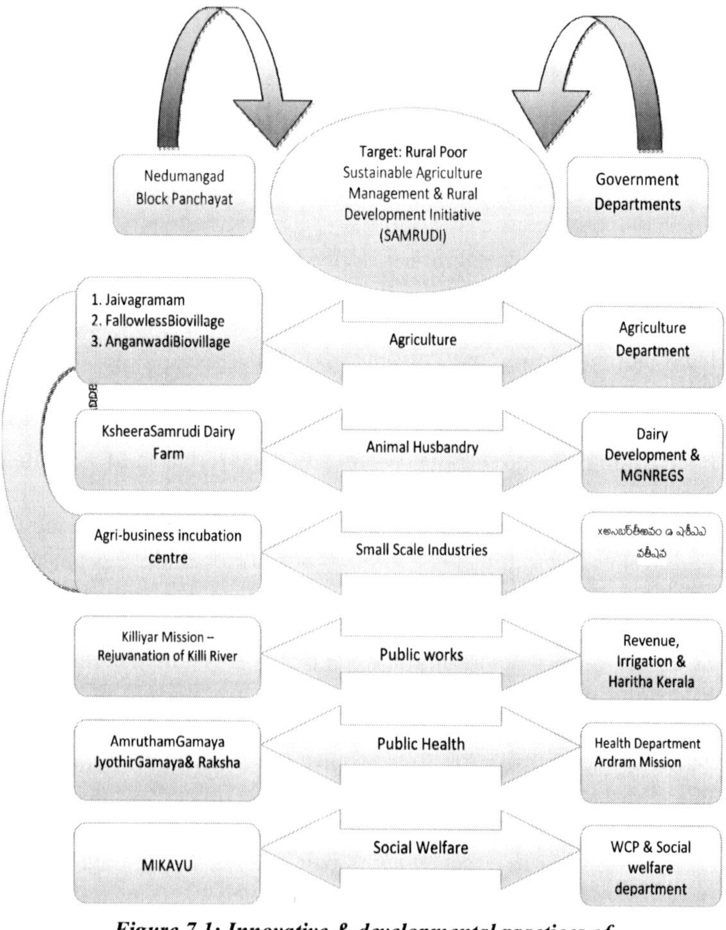

Figure 7.1: Innovative & developmental practices of Nedumangad Block Panchayat (2016-17 to 2018-19)

collaboration with the five-gram Panchayaths under the block's jurisdiction. It is noteworthy that the participation is observed beyond political dimensions and diverging philosophies. Linkages at the top end is observed wherein the Block Panchayath efficiently implements the state schemes and policies by drawing from the expertise of state departments and its functionaries. Funds from various schemes were appropriately channelized and agriculture development was viewed as a path to rural self-sufficiency and independence. The schemes like Jyothirgamaya Balya and Kaumara are adopted at district level and is recognised as a tested model.

Secondly, the Block Panchayaths are structured by statute enabling convergence among various tiers and other departments at state level. This aid appropriate channelizing of funds and utilisation of expertise by various agencies. Nedumangad Block Panchayath, through its various projects and interventions has successfully established a convergence. By convergence, the Block has enabled effective utilisation of technical expertise at all levels and the possibility of grass root level penetration of the village level administration. The specifications of the best and innovative practices in selected developmental areas of Nedumangad Block Panchayaths is given in figure 7.1.

Thirdly, most of the projects and schemes that the Block Panchayath has formulated and implemented have a direct or indirect bearing upon the productive sectors. This is an important feature as most Block Panchayaths fail wherein service sector schemes that the village level administration can easily coordinate is replicated at block level. Agriculture is identified as the pivot of interventions, the local economy being essentially agrarian in nature. A new dimension to the sector was made by incorporating and popularising organic cultivation among the residents. A model Bio village was set up to present to the public the viability of organic farming. Further, farm knowledge was disseminated through indigenous farmers and authorities to the identified agents of change, particularly children. The success in agriculture further trickles down to the other sectors like rural industries and public health, wherein agro-based industries were set up so as to reduce post-harvest loss and to motivate rural entrepreneurs and safe to eat practices were embarked as foundation to good public health. Infrastructural policies were founded on the principle of circular economy, wherein wastage is minimised and resources are capitalised optimally.

Fourthly, tracing the development areas of Nedumangad Block Panchayaths, it is observed that they make a chain of interventions, sequential in nature. Primary interventions were made in promoting the productive sectors of the local economy, which has direct benefits to the community. Consequently agriculture, animal husbandry and Agri Business units were opened up. Simultaneously, in social service front, public health that has maximum community spill over was emphasised. Within the health care sector, activities were so formulated as to cater the vulnerable groups and in creating awareness about cancer- the most prominent non-communicable disease in the state. Further, the spectrum of interventions widened, adopting Killiyar mission which envisioned renewing Killi river with people's participation. All these activities were grounded on the cultural and historical fabric of the locality, thereby adhering to the spirit of decentralisation.

Fifthly, all the interventions by the Nedumangad Block Panchayath were made with a big picture of sustainability, conceived at economic, social and environmental front. All practices can be found to come under the purview of environmental governance with sustainable resource management and strengthening, with the aim to manage individual behaviors and motivating collective actions in pursuance of public environmental goods and related societal outcomes In a decentralised social contexts, environmental governance addresses diverse issues at a range of scales and at the level of implementation by the block; strengthening and managing natural resources is a socio-ecological and participatory sustainable development process targeting enhanced livelihood status of the rural poor, encompassing the attributes of robustness, responsiveness, equity and effectiveness; determining the practicability and sustainability of outcomes. Here a responsive and robust machinery ensures that environmental governance is adaptable both to dynamic conditions and to diverse contexts that exemplify: learning, anticipation, adaptability, innovation, and flexibility. Further it is observed that the philosophy and intentions underlying the interventions of Nedumanagd Block Panchayath is robust– persisting over time, maintaining performance, and coping with perturbations and crises, being legitimate, connected, nested, and polycentric.

Sixthly, the interventions at all level are equitable and founded on the merits of collective action. Equitable governance begins with policies and processes that recognize, respect, and are inclusive of the perspectives, knowledge systems, values, cultures, and rights of diverse stakeholders (Borrini-Feyerabend et al., 2015; Lockwood et al., 2010; McDermott, Mahanty, &Schreckenberg, 2013), including the views of groups who are the ultimate beneficiaries. In this sense, fostering collective action can go a long way perpetuating the decentralized structure of resource management and augmenting local specific resources. It is observed that the Nedumangad Block Panchayath has brought together the organizational arrangements and institutional arrangements of collective action through proper planning, management and monitoring, to make the development interventions successful.

Seventhly, Block Panchayath level administration is vehemently criticised for its lack of own fund creation and therefore the shrinking role as mere facilitator. However, Nedumangad Block Panchayath has developed its own prospects for own fund creation, as the outcome of the various schemes put forward by it. The initiatives like Jaivagramam, RRF and Agri Business Incubation Center are projects with prospects for own fund creation.Preliminary investments were made in these sectors, that will aid long run benefits and income. Jaivagramam and the associated projects on agricultural front today has a wider market share within the locality and across the state, contributing to the own fund of the Block. RRF once fully operationalized would amass a profit out of selling shredded and pressed plastics to the Clean Kerala Company, after covering the labour costs and operational expenses. Similarly, the Agri Business Incubation Centre offers handholding services and machines to the trained entrepreneurs by charging a nominal user fee, which is also to the credit of Block Panchayath. Apart from the user fee, the Block Panchayath targets to create a brand under SAMRUDHI for the various value-added products, which will smoothen the marketing process and would be a source of income for the Block Panchayath.

Finally, the success of Nedumangad Block Panchayath shall be attributed to the political will and ability of administrative construct in identifying agents of change in all development areas. Women were identified as primary beneficiaries of several projects in productive sectors. This is from the spirit that income of women is ultimately an investment in child care and social change. Children were carefully capitalised as vehicles for carrying forward the change to future. They are sensitised of the need for having a good health and safe to eat crops. These efforts ultimately make the Block Panchayathself-reliant.

The development experience of Nedumangad Block Panchayath is identified by the study as a success model which has replicable merits under the framework integrating concepts of Good Governance, Environmental Governance and sustainability. The study is based on the four-year period since 2015, which has made remarkable changes to the institution, its performance and outcomes. It is understood that the success is rooted in the local body, functioning in alignment with the statutory functions, that has enabled Nedumanagad Block Panchayath to foster adequate backward and forward linkages and utilise the technical expertise of governmental and non-governmental agencies in formulating and implementing policies in various sectors. These linkages facilitated identification of best practices that ultimately optimises resource utilisation, by strengthening resource base, managing natural resources and creating sustainable livelihood. All the interventions, aligning to the statutory delegated functions are rooted in the larger purview of Good Environmental Governance, recognising that sustainable development initiatives occur at the local level and good governance is based on the identification of individuals and institutions that should be empowered to make decisions about natural resources and their management. The block initially strengthened the structures in order to enable the body to fully assume the role as facilitators of sustainable development. Local residents were empowered as to not only share the benefits arising from the use of natural resources, but also participate in decisions regarding resource management and the power of collective action was utilised. It is observed from the study that in decentralised social contexts, efficient execution of constitutional visions and environmental governance with a long term perspective for diverse issues and range of scales can have remarkable imprints and in adherence to the above mentioned concept and praxis; Nedumangad Block Panchayath remains as a Block with replicable merits, providing testimony to the relevance of Block Panchayaths as change agents in the decentralised system of governance.

Appendices

Appendix - 1

Mikavu

The local governments were mandated to develop infrastructure for cultural performances and sports activities; to widen the accessibility to cultural goods and services, and to ensure that culture reinforces the reflection of their regions. The local governments cannot directly manage and control activities resulting from many changing interactions. However, they can care about the quality of their environment and insert the incentives that will induce both creativity and accountability. They need to understand communities, not just of those who are already visible, but also those who live in the margins or who use the place occasionally. The progressive social changes in Kerala have affected the growth of art forms as well. Every effort is to be made to reform art forms with a view tomeeting the needs of are formed and changing society and making it attractive and enjoyable to the common people of all communities andclasses.

In recognition of the importance of traditional arts and to ensure its growth at a sustainable level, the initiatives are intended to address the existing structural limitations of the sector and meet the needs of the community practicing traditional arts. The practice of traditional art forms is deeply skill-based. However, over the years the space that the traditional art forms in Kerala has had is exhibiting a declining trend. This is compounded by a general lack of teaching, research and documentation as well as limited platforms for critical discourse on traditional art forms. There is a pressing need to address these issues; to motivate participation, to develop appreciation and

Appendix - 2

Social Audit

The process of decentralisation and the evaluation at beneficiary end is widely performed through various internal and statutory audit mechanisms. However, among the various evaluation practices; social audit stands out for its multiple dimensions; being participatory, self-deterministic and holistic. Social Audit is a process by which citizens of the locality, who are beneficiaries of development and welfaristic interventions of their respective local body, evaluate the performance of the varied schemes of which they are beneficiaries themselves and assess the spill over benefits. Nedumangad block envisages to conduct a social audit of 10 major sustainable and innovative projects undertaken by the block over the past four years. Shri B Biju, President of Nedumangad Block Panchayath coordinated the initiative and guidance from experts including Dr. T.M. Issac (Hon'ble Finance Minister, Kerala), Prof. K.N. Harilal (Member, State Planning Board) were sought. The specific schemes and strategies subject to social audit were:

1. Sustainable Agricultural Management and Rural Development Initiatives (SAMRUDHI), for capitalising the potential of Agriculture in the block.
2. Vallamnira, a project for nutritional self-sufficiency at household level
3. Jaivagramam, a model Bio village reiterating organic practices

4. Jyothirgamayabalya, ensuring preventive and curative care for children
5. JyothirgamayaKaumara, giving health education, social orientation and health care facilities for young adults and parents.
6. Maramath, Strengthening infrastructural base through Public works
7. Killiyar Protection, extending the activities of block to rejuvenation of Killi river through participatory approach
8. Agri-Incubation Centre, providing training and support to women entrepreneurs in Agri-food processing sector
9. Projects strengthening the socio-cultural fabrics of the locality and creating sustainable livelihoods
10. General opinion of public on Development and Policy execution through convergence of line departments by the block.

A scientific and inclusive methodology was adopted, and foremost, Social Audit committees were formed at various levels for developing appropriate tools, coordinating field visits, volunteers and experts, conducting observation walks and monitoring group discussions. The procedures and tentative findings were periodically discussed and analysed. Such formed groups of volunteers and experts, collected data from beneficiaries pertaining to implementation of each project, opinion on functionaries and suggestions for change. Further, a special committee of Grama Sabha was convened and findings were presented for feedback and the draft report was presented before a jury at Block level Jana Sabha, comprising social activist Aruna Roy (Director of the Society for Social Audits Accountability and Transparency (SSAAT), Soumya Kidambi and former Chief Secretary S.M. Vijayanand. The draft report analysed the level of accomplishment of each project against its proposed vision of socio-economic and environmental sustainability and discussed the continuity, consistency and future prospects. In addition to the apparent lessons, the exercise was an evaluation of Local Self Governance and its ability to converge different departments for grass root level interventions.

Appendix - 3

Abhayam

The award money received by Nedumangad Block Panchayath in recognition to its various developmental initiatives, over its tenure from 2016-17, is planned to be channelized to palliative care under an innovative scheme 'Abhayam', an extension of the broader SAMRUDHI project. Nedumangad Panchayath is the proud recipient of many prestigious awards including the Deen Dayal Upadhyay Panchayath Sasakthikaran Puraskar for its outstanding efforts and initiatives, consecutively during 2017-18 and 2018-19, Swaraj Trophy during 2017-18 and 2018-19, Prathibha Puraskar for excellence in performance of Block Panchayath president during2017-18, award for best performance in health sector innovative approach from Ayush International Conclave during 2017-18 and for the best ATMA Group from Department of Agriculture, Kerala in 2016-17, the prize money accounting for a total of eighty lakhs rupees.

The project 'Abhayam' intends to create a corpus fund with the award money along with voluntary charity contributions and CSR fund, and further to invest this amount with cooperative bank. The project is conceived in such a way as to benefit bedridden and terminally ill patients with primary priority to cancer patients (per month provision of approximately 750 INR/1000 INR). The beneficiaries of the scheme would be identified by the general committee of the Block Panchayath from the list provided by respective Grama Panchayaths and the amount would be credited to the zero balance accounts of the beneficiaries. The Committee consisting of Block Panchayath President, BDO, Standing Committee Chairman of Health and Education, Planning Committee Vice Chairman and VEO of respective Gram Panchayaths; will be monitoring the scheme by conducting timely visit to these patients at regular fixed intervals. The subsequently elected Block authorities can further strengthen the scheme by devoting plan fund to palliative care. The project intends to have rippled effects over time and is expected to be one of the unique and pertinent welfare schemes of Nedumangad Block Panchayath, since it is the first of its kind where a local self-government body is utilising the award money with greater humanitarian and social outlook.

References

B A Prakash et.al. 2013. Effectiveness of Service Delivery in Panchayat Raj Institutions in Kerala. RGIDS and NIRD.

Bennett, Nathan J., and Terre Satterfield.2018. Environmental Governance: A Practical Framework to Guide Design, Evaluation, and Analysis. Conservation Letters. Accessed 19.02.2020. https://doi.org/10.1111/conl.12600.

Bennett, Nathan J., Lydia Teh, Yoshitaka Ota, Patrick Christie, Adam Ayers, Jon C. Day, Phil Franks, et al.2017. An Appeal for a Code of Conduct for Marine Conservation. Marine Policy. Accessed 19.02.2020 https://doi.org/10.1016/j.marpol.2017.03.035.

Bennett, Nathan, and Terre Satterfield. Environmental Governance: A Practical Framework to Guide Design, Evaluation, and Analysis. 2018. Accessed 19.02.2020 https://doi.org/10.31230/osf.io/n2ahd.

Eaton, Kent.2011.The Political Economy of Decentralization Reforms: Implications for Aid Effectiveness. The World Bank. Accessed 19.02.2020 https://doi.org/10.1596/978-0-8213-8840-2.

Government of Kerala (2009): Report of the Committee for Evaluation of Decentralised Planning and Development (Thrissur: Kerala Institute of Local Administration).

Graham, John, Bruce Amos, and Tim Plumptre.2003. Governance Principles for Protected Areas in the 21st Century.Governance Principles for Protected AreasInstitute on Governance, Canada.

Jha, Shikha. 2004. Panchayats – Functions, Responsibilities and Resources. Accessed 07.09. 2019.https://www.researchgate.net/publication/259384810_Panchayats_-_Functions_Responsibilities_and_Resources/link/54f2e01f0cf24eb87949b6cf/download.

Lockwood, Michael. 2010. Good Governance for Terrestrial Protected Areas: A Framework, Principles and Performance Outcomes. Journal of Environmental Management.Accessed19.02.2020 https://doi.org/10.1016/j.jenvman.2009.10.005.

Madhava Menon N.R.2016. Inter governmental Relations and Constitutional Governance in Panchayatiraj Experience in India, Raman Pillai K. , Suresh Kumar R.K and Sukumaran Nair P (eds), Kalpaz publications, Delhi.

Mcdermott, Melanie, Sango Mahanty, and Kate Schreckenberg. 2013. Examining Equity: A Multidimensional Framework for Assessing Equity in Payments for Ecosystem Services. Environmental Science & Policy. Accessed 19.02.2020 https://doi.org/10.1016/j.envsci.2012.10.006.

Oommen T K.1984. Social Transformation in Rural India: Mobilization and State Intervention. Vikas. University of California.

Pascual, Unai, Jacob Phelps, EnekoGarmendia, Katrina Brown, EsteveCorbera, Adrian Martin, Erik Gomez-Baggethun, and Roldan Muradian. 2014. Social Equity Matters in Payments for Ecosystem Services. BioScience. Accessed 19.02.2020https://doi.org/10.1093/biosci/biu146.

Prakash et al. (2013) Effectiveness of Service delivery in Panchayat Raj Institutions, RGIDS, Thiruvananthapuram.

P.T. Thomas. 2016. Fiscal Decentralization and Economic Development: The Kerala Experience. Notion Press:India. Accessed 29.08.2019. https://notionpress.com/read/fiscal-decentralisation-and-economic-development-the-kerala-experience

Reed, Mark S. 2008. Stakeholder Participation for Environmental Management: A Literature Review. Biological Conservation. 19.02.2020 https://doi.org/10.1016/j.biocon.2008.07.014.

S M Vijayanand. 2009. Kerala – A Case Study Of Classical Democratic Decentralization. Kerala Institute of Local Administration (KILA). Accessed 07.09.2019. https://www.panchayatgyan.gov.in/documents.

Tulia G. Falleti. 2005. A Sequential Theory of Decentralization: Latin American Cases in Comparative Perspective. Cambridge University Press. Accessed 25.08.2019. https://doi.org/10.1017/S0003055405051695.

Angelo Bonfiglioli. 2004. Lands of the Poor: Local Environmental Governance and the Decentralized Management of Natural Resources. UNCDF. Accessed 19.02. 2020. https://b-ok.org/book/1083798/371d62.

Zafra-Calvo, N., U. Pascual, D. Brockington, B. Coolsaet, J. A. Cortes-Vazquez, N. Gross-Camp, I. Palomo, and N. D. Burgess. 2017. Towards an Indicator System to Assess Equitable Management in Protected Areas. Biological Conservation.Accessed 19.02.2020 https://doi.org/10.1016/j.biocon.2017.05.014.

Index

H

I

J

K

L

M

N

O

P

R

S